American Blackness

American Blackness

Navigating the Myth of the Black Monolith

Bernard Grenway

HAMILTON BOOKS
Lanham • Boulder • New York • London

Published by Hamilton Books
An imprint of The Rowman & Littlefield Publishing Group, Inc.
4501 Forbes Boulevard, Suite 200, Lanham, Maryland 20706
www.rowman.com

6 Tinworth Street, London SE11 5AL, United Kingdom

Copyright © 2021 The Rowman & Littlefield Publishing Group, Inc.

All rights reserved. No part of this book may be reproduced in any form or by any electronic or mechanical means, including information storage and retrieval systems, without written permission from the publisher, except by a reviewer who may quote passages in a review.

British Library Cataloguing in Publication Information Available

Library of Congress Control Number:

Names: Grenway, Bernard, author.
Title: American Blackness : navigating the myth of the Black monolith / Bernard Grenway.
Other titles: Navigating the myth of the Black monolith
Description: Lanham : Hamilton Books, [2021] | Includes index. | Summary: "This book uses theoretical applications and social narratives to push back against ideals associated with of the black monolith by examining the many ways in which black Americans struggle to cope with educational, cultural, and socio-economical expectations"—Provided by publisher.
Identifiers: LCCN 2021021643 (print) | LCCN 2021021644 (ebook) | ISBN 9780761872559 (paperback) | ISBN 9780761872566 (ebook)
Subjects: LCSH: Grenway, Bernard. | African Americans—Biography. | United States—Race relations—Anecdotes. | African Americans—Social conditions—1975-
Classification: LCC E185.97.G797 A3 2021 (print) | LCC E185.97.G797 (ebook) | DDC 305.896/0730904—dc23
LC record available at https://lccn.loc.gov/2021021643
LC ebook record available at https://lccn.loc.gov/2021021644

Contents

1	Little Black Boy, Big White Suburbia	1
2	Six Black Boys in a Room	9
3	Out-Black Me: The Unwinnable Game of Black Male Success	11
4	You Love Who You Love, Race Notwithstanding	21
5	The Truth about Blackness: Navigating Free Black Will	25
6	Ink Black and Rail Thin	27
7	Dubois Talks about That Twoness	29
8	Lessons of a Mixed-Race Family: You Can't Have It Both Ways	31
9	For Those Who Overlook What Really Happened	37
10	Racial Reality Intelligence: The Truth Will Set America Free	39
11	That Ceremonial Covering That is Me	43
12	Afroprovidential Redirection: That Force That Steps into the Gap	45
13	An Early Discernment: Racial Categorization	55
14	Transformation: A Discussion of Displaced Adulation	57
15	Black the Way I Want to Be	71

16	The Learning of Racial Mythologies and the DNA Conundrum: Are You Sure You're White?	73
17	The Employee Paradox: Respecting the Psychology of Black Workmanship	81
18	The Ascension of Desires Continuum: What Maslow Forgot to Tell You about Black Working People	87
19	America's Dissociation Identity Disorder: Fearing the Blackness of Obama Part I	95
20	America's Dissociation Identity Disorder: Fearing the Blackness of Obama Part II: Trapped in the Throes of White Narcissism	111
21	A Morning on Poplar Grove	115
22	My Visceral Heartbeat: The Hip-Hop Side of Me	117
Index		121
About the Author		127

Chapter One

Little Black Boy, Big White Suburbia

I have this memory that keeps coming back to me. It interrupts the monotony of my adulthood like a familiar visitor. It's repetitive. It has attached itself to my soul as if it were a cognitive limb—a connected piece of mind-flesh that moves when I move. I can almost feel its arm around my neck, pulling me closer to myself. Its warm breath slithers into my inner ear and pushes past the hammer and the anvil. It glides beyond the cochlea and burrows into my consciousness.

The memory originates from the early 1980s. I was a ten-year-old little brown boy with milk white eyes, undersized running shorts, and ashen knees. I was new, just a beginner in the labyrinth of life. I was wearing white tube socks stretched along my skinny shins, and my hair was a black bedraggled mop of tight, nappy curls. It was jungle-thick and tangled. I was resting in a patch of summer grass. I inhaled the scent of tall fescue and wilting dandelion. I could feel the droplets of youthful sweat taking residence in the crevice of my puerile armpits. The aroma of male adolescence was on me. It was dank and abundant. The sun was massive; it dangled heavily from God's string. It seemed close enough to touch, and as I rested on my back, digging my fingers into the sunburnt carpet of weeds and green flora, the summer heat enveloped me: ninety-four degrees and climbing. Dry, hot, and blazing in waves of yellow, the rays hovered above me until they turned my skin an even deeper shade of chocolate ochre. It cooked to the core.

Turning on my side, I was filled with contentment, but I couldn't help wondering what the day held. Where would the moment lead me? There was something monumental in the air—something new. But at that moment, I was locked in the midst of a lazy June day that permeated my Maryland suburbia and separated my future epochs. I was just a few miles away from the D.C. streets where I would one day go to high school, just a few miles away from the Baltimore streets where I would one day spend my summers, just a few miles away from everything and anything that was real and dangerous, that was alive and threatening—the ensuing zeitgeist that was a black boy's unwritten future.

Unable to resist the constant swarming of mosquitoes and yellowjackets that flew above my widened eyes, I bounced promptly to my feet. I was light on my toes—cat-quick. In an instant, I was walking. I was dragging the laces of my untied sneakers through a maze of leaf-covered bike paths and oddly shaped backyards. The laces seemed to attract grassy residue, picking up fallen leaves within the frays. The yards zipped by as I moved. Some had fences, while others were open, giving way to matching lawn sets and sun-stained decks. Stepping over broken branches fallen from a previous storm, I followed the summer wind heating the playgrounds and unused grills. I was heading nowhere with the full intent of dwelling in the moment, a black pubescent nomad, a child of the world. I was lost in reverie.

As I walked, I saw a female jogger with tight, straight lips and a flat jaw. She was bounding toward me. The muscles in her legs convulsed with every stride, twitching like blinking eyes. Her movements were fluid. She was streamlined. Her hair, straight and jet black, was pasted to her scalp. It almost looked plastic, as if it were painted on her head. She was drenched in sweat. The sunlight broke into shattered fragments through the trees. I noticed her beauty. Her symmetry was astounding. She smiled as she ran by me. Her shoes crunched rhythmically in the gravel and grass, much like a metronome, in perfect sequence. I peered into her eyes as she passed, and I returned the favor, showing the whiteness of my teeth. I caught a close glimpse of her face. The irises of her eyes were delicate. They were soft and watery, yet there was a cool sternness about them, a feline seriousness. My mind told me they were also filled with questions. They were eyes housing a multitude of queries: *Whose little black boy is this? Does he live around here? Where is he going? Should I run on the other side of the path?*

As she slipped past me, she took her silent queries and sweat-covered body along. I fought the urge to turn around. Her scent hung in the air; it grew fingers that reached toward me, fingers that tugged at the puberty within me. The sound of her footsteps disappeared as the distance grew between us. I began to move on. My eyes were forward. She was well beyond my reach.

Before long, I came to a collection of single-family homes with manicured front yards and square walkways. The lawns were prim and proper. The houses seemed to be related. They shared DNA, birthed via the same architectural womb by builders and designers who sought to cultivate the quintessential suburban experience . . . middle class, middle of the world, middle of the pack, middle of suburbia. It was an experience permeated with matching silverware and potpourri, electronic garage doors, a collection of green water hoses (which always seemed to get wrapped around a flattened soccer ball and the morning paper) the melodic chanting of crickets, willow trees, and summer insects. Roads were lined with dwellings in which the two cars in the driveway were European square Volvos, rounded Peugeots, and Volkswagens. The lawns were scattered with flower beds teeming with snapdragons and store-purchased topsoil and chocolate-colored mulch. There was the chirping of birds I could not name. There were American flags on poles, Baltimore Orioles flags on poles, a few Confederate flags on poles. *Don't tread on me.* And then there was me. A black spot mislaid in a world that was simultaneously full and devoid of color. I kept moving, heading on. As I eased into a cul-de-sac, I saw a familiar face. My heart tingled. His name was Chris. We both attended the neighborhood elementary school located at the top of the hill. In the suburbs, it seemed like every elementary school was located at the top of a hill.

Chris smiled when he saw me and urged me to come toward his house. As I approached, I caught a glimpse of his eyes. They were cat-shaped, and they shimmered a deep, penetrating, and shocking cerulean blue. His eyes were the kind of blue that reminded me of sapphire birthstones. They rolled like soft ocean foam when he smiled. His skin was pale, and a collection of haphazard freckles competed for the real estate between his forehead and chin. The freckles didn't stop at his face; they seemed to spread down his arms like a patch of roving camouflage. As I got closer, I was amazed at how aesthetically different we were. We were the inverse of one another—alabaster versus onyx, the chosen versus the invisible. His body was small and fleshy. I was stout and powerful. His skin burned in the summer sun. My body soaked up rays as if it could taste them. He was moonstone. I was obsidian. Despite the outer differences, the child within brought us together as one.

We were thrilled to see one another. I rushed to his side and exclaimed I did not know he lived on that street. Chris hugged me and then slapped me five. The smack echoed throughout the cul-de-sac. The ocean foam in his eyes rolled again. I rolled with it. For a second, I was seasick. We laughed until we doubled over—ten-year-old nirvana.

In an instant, Chris grabbed my elbow and led me over to his driveway. There was a basketball hoop in front of his house. It was rusted with sandbags that held down the base. I happily followed his lead. Chris picked up a tattered basketball and thrusted it into my chest. It made a hollow thud when it hit my sternum. The ball was damp from a previous rainstorm and smelled like a wet dog. The leather was worn. I squeezed it tightly. It felt familiar in my hands as if it were my very own, as if it were connected to my nervous system, fused with my axons and dendrites. As I dribbled the ball the first few times, my talent was obvious. The ball appeared to be on a string, rising and falling like a yo-yo. Chris backed up and stooped into a defensive stance. He slid his tongue to the side of his mouth, and the freckles on his face seemed to reconfigure. Despite his intense concentration, I glided past and beyond him with ease, teasing him with the ball. I bounced it between my legs as I had done a thousand times before in my front yard. I dribbled it behind my back as I had done in my little league games, traveling team games, and my all-star games . . . so many games. The sport always came effortlessly to me—as natural as sleeping.

Chris stumbled over his feet as I dribbled. His legs were stiff. He moved as though his feet sprouted roots. His heels became one with the concrete pulling him downward, slowing him, grounding him. In a flash, I spun around and dashed toward the basket. He trailed in my wake, and although my eyes were fixed on the rim, I saw Chris trailing me from the corner of my eye. I saw him trying to dislodge the weights that bound him to pavement. I saw the grimace on his face, the azure-blue roll of his ocean eyes. Still eyeing the rim, I took two quick steps and flipped the ball into the hoop. It made a rattling sound as it fell through the basket. I smiled. Chris smiled as well.

"I forgot you never miss," he said, sighing.

At that moment, a larger boy emerged from Chris's house. The boy's shoulders were wide, and his hair hung like a stringed chandelier down the whiteness of his back. His movements were slow and cumbersome, and although he shared Chris's camouflage freckles and ocean-blue eyes, his expression was fixed into a scowl. It rested on his face like a broken mask. The boy jumped down the front steps, bounding two at a time, and made his way over to me. My back tightened. I froze in my tracks.

"Who is this?" the boy asked as he scanned me from head to toe.

"That's Bernard," Chris answered, still breathing hard from the basketball game. "He's in my class. We're both in Mr. Weech's class."

The larger boy moved closer and yanked the ball from my hands. I tried to hold on, but I was overwhelmed by his strength. Chris eased over and sat on the front steps. Our eyes locked.

"Mr. Weech is a black nigger faggot," the boy retorted, still holding the ball in his freckled hands. I glanced at Chris for help. He lowered his head and explained, in a sullen tone, that the larger boy was his brother.

I forced a smile in the hope I could break the tension. The grease in the larger boy's hair shone in the sun. It looked as if it had not been washed for weeks. His face was covered with acne. His lips were tight. A few stubbles of blond hair pushed through the skin beneath his chin. His shorts were cut-off jeans, and an assemblage of frayed denim strings hung down from where scissors had cut them. His boots were black with untied laces, and when he walked, one could see the powerful firmness of his legs. I found myself reaching for the ball, and I could smell the remnants of cigarettes on his breath.

I wanted the ball back. I needed the familiarity of its roundness. I needed to feel the safety it provided, the feelings of home. The boy sensed my desire and allowed a tilted smile to flicker on his face.

"Oh, you want this?" he shouted. I nodded and stretched my arms toward the ball. "I tell you what," he continued, "I will play you for the ball. If you win, you can take it."

In an instant, two other boys emerged from the house and sat on the front step. I assumed from the lack of blueness in their eyes they were not related to Chris, but I wasn't sure.

Seconds later, the game began. Chris's brother took the ball and stumbled past me. His movements were robotic, slow, metallic, and predictable. He was cumbersome like Chris, and his feet seemed to grow roots. As he pushed forward, I slapped the ball from his hands, grabbed it, and glided backward as I dribbled between my legs. The two older boys on the steps laughed mockingly. I could feel a surge in my confidence. An inferno blazed in my opponent's eyes. As he lunged forward, I smoothly flipped the ball behind my back and shot a lazy hook. The ball rattled around the rim and fell through the basket.

"One to zip," I blurted proudly. The boys on the step laughed. Chris's brother walked toward me.

"Don't do that again," he said.

The warmth from his breath wafted into my face. I pretended not to hear him, and as the game continued, I danced around him as if he weren't there. As if he were a figment of my puerile imagination—a ghost. He reached for the ball, and I moved it to my left hand. He lunged again, and I switched it into my right hand. He came toward me, and I retreated, spun, and slid the ball between my legs yet again. The yo-yo was fully operational, and before long, the score was seven to nothing.

One of the older boys lit a cigarette and rose to his feet. He leaned his scrawny white body against the rail near the steps and shook the hair from his face. "That little black kid's kickin' your fuckin' ass," he blurted. "He's like six years younger than you, dude."

Chris giggled under his breath. I smiled nervously, admiring the compliment. Chris's brother rolled his eyes. They began to look more like storms than oceans. I held the ball tightly. I prepared, once again, to dribble, but when I bounced the ball, Chris's brother raised his right hand and cracked me on the side of my face. It felt like a flash of white heat. The pain spread into a splintered fissure that leaked into the crevices of my nose and cheek. A rainbow of colors filled the watery spaces in my eyes. The summer light became blurred, and for a second, the world was a meandering, spinning kaleidoscope—a contorted throng of backward yellows and capsized fuchsias, slanted greens, and upturned purples. The driveway seemed to rise, slamming into the side of my head. Everything echoed. I struggled to get to my feet, but the pounding on the side of my head grew with every breath. Chimes rang. My balance was off-kilter. I scrambled backward and pushed myself up into a stooped position, watching as the blood from my nose dripped in burgundy puddles along the driveway. I stood upright and steadied my stance. The larger boy came after me again. His hair flung wildly. His grin was devilish. I noticed the crooked spaces in his teeth. I ducked his haymaker and backed up a few feet. I could hear the giggles of the boys on the steps. My fists were clenched. I fought back tears.

Chris screamed out, "Stop it, Mike! Stop it! Bernard is my friend."

"Shut the hell up, Chris," his brother retorted.

I placed the ball on the driveway and backed away slowly, never taking my eyes off Chris's brother's face. It widened out into a joker's sinister grin. The ball rolled into the neighbor's yard. The large boy walked back over to the steps and sat down. His chest heaved, and I could see the thickness of his torso under his black T-shirt. He extracted a pack of cigarettes from his right pocket and slid one into the corner of his mouth. He lit it and brushed the hair from his face. He puffed a stream of gray smoke into the summer air. I continued walking backward.

"Where you going you, little black nigger?" he shouted. I remained silent and kept backing away. "You know that's what you are, right?" he continued. "Just a little, ugly, black fuckin' nigger boy with nappy hair and jungle lips." The kids on the step continued to laugh. "That's all you'll ever be. Go ahead, run home! You ugly fuckin' nigger boy! You little black faggot!"

Before long, I realized I had backed all the way out of the cul-de-sac. So far that I could barely see the expressions on their faces. I could see only the outlines of their bodies sitting on the steps, watching me retreat. As I turned the corner, I began to jog. My heart swelled with each step. The jog transmuted, quickly, into a full-fledged sprint back along the bike paths and oddly shaped yards, beyond the broken branches, and past playgrounds with unused grills. The frayed laces on my untied shoes whipped the skin on my legs, and my heart pounded in unison with my acceleration. Tears fell from my eyes and mixed with the blood from my nose. I continued to run, faster and faster. I ran in anger, pain, and embarrassment. I passed the female jogger as she progressed toward her starting point. We flashed by one other. I could see her moving to the other side of the street as if she were afraid. She noticed the blood and tears dripping from my face, the frantic look in my tear-filled eyes. I grimaced as we passed one another. She picked up her pace and turned down an adjacent pathway. Once again, she was gone.

    The anger grew in my core, surging up my body until I stopped and bent over. Vomit pushed up my throat and covered the grassy space between my feet. I wiped my mouth with the backside of my hand and began to run again. As I ran, I felt the burning rage build in my body. All I wanted to do was get bigger, get stronger, get older so I could return to Chris's house and punch his brother in the mouth to get back my self-respect—to stake my claim. As I rounded the hill leading to my home, my sprint slowed to a jog again, then to a walk. The ache on the side of my face continued to sting. My heartbeat slowed, and I wondered what would happen the next time I'd be called that word. I'd be ready the next time. Next time, I would be ready—maybe?

Chapter Two

Six Black Boys in a Room

We were sitting in a huddle—cramped, stuffed inside a teenager's bedroom. Tube socks and video game cartridges were strewn across the knotted carpet. It was a broken-down row home with stray dogs barking outside the window. Our backs were bent, all six of us with our elbows on our knees, sitting on the bed, our faces downward.

Music played, bass pulsating through the room. The lyrics were difficult to make out due to speaker distortion. Every other word was a curse word. All six of us bobbed our heads to the beat with scowls on our faces. The room reeked of underarms and incense. Funk and cannabis.

The bedroom door flew open. A boy walked in. He was tall and lean. His jeans were frayed, his sneakers were white, a green bandana struggled to restrain his dreadlocks. He smiled, exposing his gold teeth and high cheekbones. We nodded to the boy. He sat on the bed next to us and reached into his jacket pocket. He pulled out a gun, and the sunlight from the window reflected off the chrome; it blinked in the rays. He ran his hands along the barrel and rose to his feet. Grasping the gun, he pretended to shoot. One eye closed. His arm extended. The gun slanted sideways.

There was a noise outside on the street. Three of the boys leaned over toward the window to see police cars pull up. The officers spilled out of their cars like a steady and deliberate blue wax. They saw the police pick up their pace as they entered the house via the front door. Time quickened.

The boys panicked, eyes as wide as silver dollars. They scattered in various directions, knocking over the television, which fell to the floor. I ran out into the hallway to see the officers bounding up the stairs. I watched the twists of their mouths as they leapt two steps at a time. A curse left my mouth in a whisper. The officers gained traction. One of the teenagers got caught. I heard him cursing, too.

Chapter Two

   I sprinted to the bathroom and pushed my way inside. I stepped over the toilet and squeezed my body through the bathroom window. I was hanging halfway out. It was a ten-foot drop to the alley. I pushed all the way through. I was falling, headfirst. The alley floor was rising quickly. I somehow contorted my body so my feet and hands hit the concrete at the same time, catlike, on all fours. The pain flashed as I landed, stunned. Wobbly, I tried to stand. I began to run, but my limp slowed me down. I ran away from the sirens. I could hear my raspy breathing. I could hear my feet hitting the concrete, three blocks away, then four blocks away. I began to slow down and turned back onto the street. Five blocks away. I placed my aching hands in the pockets of my jeans and headed toward the subway, catching my breath. I slowed my pace. I planned my next move. I planned my next idea. I planned to stay alive.

Chapter Three

Out-Black Me

The Unwinnable Game of Black Male Success

As a soft stream of fall wind slipped through the slits of the partially open car windows, I pressed the flat of my back against the seat and allowed my fingers to rest along the leathered roundness of the steering wheel. The highway uncoiled quickly. It fanned out like an impatient serpent. It cut sharply through the plush, rusted mountains of the western Maryland countryside. The dashed lines in the center of the highway spiraled out before my eyes. The car pushed through the sun-dipped woods of black cherry and winespotted leaves. I checked my periphery, switched lanes, and forced the car forward. The engine jerked as if it were resisting a direct order. I pressed the pedal harder until the car sped forward.

Glancing out the window, I allowed my eyes to fix briefly on a meandering collection of prison road crews lining the gray asphalt. They zipped by in a streaming mass of human flesh, but time slowed down. They were piecemeal—arms, legs, and faces. The men were dressed in oversized orange jumpsuits and white running sneakers. Some wore tattered baseball caps pulled tightly over their scalps. They were holding splintered wooden rakes and iron shovels in the worn brownness of their closed fists. A dim firelight seemed to twinkle faintly in their eyes with a dying blaze. I watched their bodies moving about, grunting and swaying, pushing leaves and trash away from the roadway. They perspired in flowing droplets. They almost appeared to be dancing in slow motion as they worked—mahogany zombies, soulless sleepwalkers doing the state's dirty work, and their skin was like my own.

Tearing my eyes away from the men, I returned my gaze to the road before me. I accelerated and pushed forward into the broken fragments of sunlit dew. Until that point, it had been a good day—the kind of day that tickled with promise. Although my concentration was primarily attached to the fact that I was on my way to give a lecture on business management to a collection of wide-eyed college students, it felt good to share the space in the car with two of my favorite people—Ross and X.

Ross, who sat awkwardly in the passenger seat, was a witty, brown-skinned hulk of a man with long legs, square shoulders, and an enormous belly. The flesh of his body seemed to envelop the seat, covering the vinyl as if it didn't exist. Ross hunched toward the dashboard and kept his eyes straight. Notwithstanding his desire to appear comfortable, it was evident he was not. He placed his brown hands on his knees and tried to readjust his 380 pounds and size fourteen shoes to one side or the other. The car shifted as he moved. Taking my eyes off the road and recognizing his discomfort, I leaned toward his shoulder.

"You good, Ross?" I asked, trying to reclaim the wheel. "I know this small-ass car must be killing your knees right now."

Ross lifted his darkened eyelids and shook his head slowly. The warmth of his breath and calmness of his spirit permeated the area between us. He smiled when he spoke.

"Yeah, man, I'm good. This ain't the first time I rode in a little-ass car," he blurted through a smile. "Besides, I'm happy to roll witchu, man. I appreciate the opportunity to speak to your class. It feels good to talk about my company, you know. It feels good to discuss my life's mission with college students who wanna listen. Besides, I can put this speaking gig on my resumé, right?"

I nodded and squinted into the breaking sunlight. "Hey, man, it's all good," I replied. "It's a small class, only about fifteen students or so, but they like the practical stuff. They get tired of the theory. Ya dig what I'm sayin'? Besides, it will be nice to sit down and let someone else talk for a change."

Ross leaned his wide neck against the headrest and chuckled. His stomach convulsed in unison with the rhythm of the tires.

"Yeah," he said, rubbing his hands across his rounded face. "Still, though, it must be nice to talk for a living. Hell, I might shoot for a professorship, too. Maybe I can talk for a living also. I mean, after I finish my master's."

"How long until you're done with that?" I asked, steadying the car.

A wry smile began to spread across Ross's face. I could sense the pride swelling in his core. It bubbled up to the surface. "Four months, man. Only four more months."

"I'm proud of you, man. You been working on your master's for a while now," I replied.

Exhaling and still trying to readjust his torso, Ross rolled down his window. A fresh gust of mountain air swirled inside the car. It smelled of dogwood and lilac. Ross dug into his right pocket and pulled out a stick of gum, popped it into his mouth, and glanced in my direction.

"You came a long way, Bernard," he stated, crushing the gum with his gleaming bicuspids. "Shit, I remember when you first showed up at the University of Maine. You were just a skinny kid with oversized jeans, a crooked flattop, and a basketball jones. Never thought you would become a professor. It's just crazy."

Nodding my head in agreement, I smiled, then laughed out loud. "I still can't believe it either, man. Hell, I'm just as surprised as you are. I thought I would be pumping gas or some shit, man."

"So what's the plan with your cousin?" Ross asked. "Are you gonna try and get him into school today or what? I mean, is he gonna get registered today?"

Before I could respond to Ross's inquiry, a voice from the backseat interrupted the conversation. My favorite cousin, X, chimed in. His voice was raspy and churned with flecks of gristle when he spoke. I peered into the rearview mirror as he slid upward in the seat. His eyes were puffy, and the reflection from the window ricocheted off the tan tint of his youthful skin. Although I knew X was in his twenties, I couldn't help but see the little brown boy who lived silently behind his smile. The way he retained his youth with every passing year, hibernating behind the curve of his high cheekbones and the wrangled stubble protruding from his darkened chin. X was an impressive physical specimen. His chest and arms gurgled with muscularity. His back was wide and tight. Even his forearms appeared superhuman.

"I ain't sure if they are gonna let me start school," X said, scowling. "It's the middle of the term, and they prolly' want me to fill out a bunch a paperwork and shit. I'm just sayin' . . . this trip might be a waste of time."

After a brief silence, I peered into the rearview mirror and tried to make sure our eyes met. "Come on, X," I responded. "I told you I have a few connections in the administration office. At least we can get the ball rolling, man. We can surely get you signed up for classes."

X snarled under his breath. "I know, man. I'm just sayin' this is a long way to ride for nothin'."

"Do you wanna just forget the whole thing?" I asked, still gazing at him through the rearview.

X didn't answer. He dropped his head and looked at the lint-covered floormat under his feet. A twinge of anger pulsated inside my chest. It rose like smoke up into my forehead. Although I tried to keep it at bay, I could barely conceal my disappointment. Over the past two weeks, I had allowed X to take residence in my four-year-old daughter's bedroom while she slept with my wife and me. And I had allowed him to eat my wife's cooking, use my car, spend my money, and wear my clothing. To my chagrin, X had manipulated each of the aforementioned offerings. He refused to clean my daughter's room when he awoke, leaving a scent of armpits and old cologne hanging in the air. He barely spoke to my wife, despite the fact that she had catered to his every need. He damaged my car to the tune of $350 in an unauthorized trip to a neighboring state, and as I drove closer to the campus, I was appalled at his sense of malaise. The trip, if it went well, would help him to finish up his college degree so he could get a job and take care of himself. I love him with my entire soul, but his attitude was wearing on me. I shut my mouth, drove onward, and remained quiet with eyes forward until we eventually arrived at the campus.

As we pulled in, a sense of calmness began to fill me. It traveled through my veins like a warm liquid. I loved everything about that place. I loved the aroma of freshly cut grass and Cyprus mulch. The melodic music blasting from the dorms was like an elixir, pulsating in unison—Bob Marley and Jay Z, The Doors and Kenny Chesney. I loved the familiar scent of the library and the haphazard way the students seemed to migrate in a hurry to get nowhere and everywhere at the same time as they milled about, spending their parents' money, learning to unlearn. I loved the conversations with other faculty. We'd have arguments about politics and sociology, religion and science, art and music—an intellectual's heaven. As I watched the students spill in and out of the buildings, my mind jumped back to the road crew we had passed. For in truth, the students existed in a different dimension than the black and brown men working on the road. Instead of rakes and shovels, they toted laptops and iPods.

Realizing we were early, I parked the car by a wooded section of campus. X and Ross crept out and stretched. The contrast of their bodies standing there, pushing their arms toward the sky, was a bit comical—aesthetic opposites. A thin line versus a round peg. We headed over to a collection of picnic tables perched under a large oak tree. A cool breeze fluttered about. Ross eased over and sat on the edge of the bench. It creaked as he sat down.

"So, how long before the class starts, man?" asked Ross.

"We have about an hour or so," I responded. "We can actually chill here for a bit if you want."

"Sounds good to me," Ross said. "It feels good under this tree."

X walked over to the tree and leaned his muscular back against the trunk. His skin blended with the bark, making it difficult to see where he began and the tree ended.

"I really wanna take a nap in the car," said X, "but this breeze does feel nice."

I walked over to X and stood close enough to smell the lotion on his skin. Cocoa butter. As I looked into his eyes, I saw him as a baby. The same baby I watched grow up. The same baby I envisioned as a sibling, close to my heart. More of a brother than a cousin. So much love.

"Are you ready to do this, man?" I asked with excitement. "Are you ready to get this college thing going?"

X scratched the hair on his chin and lowered his body toward the base of the tree. He stretched out his legs and picked at a blade of grass. Students and faculty, all white and smiling, rambled by us. Some disappeared into the campus buildings. Others walked around us with haste. A few waved.

X cleared his throat. "Everybody don't need to go to college, man. You think that college is for everyone." His voice tapered downward at the end of his sentence. "I really don't need a degree to do what I'm gonna do."

Ross joined in, "I hear your point, X, but you are not one of those people. You are smart enough to go to college. It will help you to get yourself on track, man."

"Yeah, man," I added, smiling at X. "You can come to this school, get the degree, and use it in the real world. It'll be easy for you, man. You're a smart dude. I know you can do it." X rose to his feet. The expression on his face seemed to change. It grew dark, storm-like.

"Why do you want everyone to act like these white people up here, man? You wanna be white, and you want every black person to be white. That's your dream, isn't it?"

A small knot began to form in my throat. "What? What are you talking about, man?" I asked. X shifted his weight and set his legs apart. For a brief instant, he looked like a black cowboy, legs bowed and arms dangling at his side, like Bill Picket or Nat Love. X's eyebrows turned downward, and a patch of wandering veins branched out on the underside of his neck. The ground seemed to rumble under his feet.

"You heard me, man!" he said a bit louder and scowled. "That's your problem. You love these white people. You worship the ground they walk on. That's your biggest problem!" A few of the smiling students turned in our direction. The hollowness of their expressions demonstrated their collective confusion.

"Yo, where is this coming from?" I asked. "Why are you talking to me like this, man?"

Ross lumbered toward X. His steps were deliberate, and I could see the concern on his face. "X," he shouted, "what the hell is wrong with you, dog? You need to respect your cousin. He's tryin' to help you, man."

X leapt forward. His hands were balled into fists, and the right side of his face seemed to quiver as he breathed. I swore he had grown at least an inch. His eyes were ablaze. They scorched like flaming coals.

"Whatever, man. Bernard is a sellout! A damn black sellout!"

Chapter Three

A rush of blood settled in my chest. I tried to force a smile, but the corners of my lips refused to budge. I'd heard X scream, but never at me. My knees trembled. A cascade of embarrassment washed over me as the students and faculty watched in silence.

"X," I shouted, "are you crazy? This ain't the place for this shit. This is my job, man."

"To hell with these white people! I don't care what they think," X exclaimed. "You fit right in here, don't you, Uncle Tom! You ain't no real nigga. You just do everything these white people want you to do. You ain't even black no more!"

Unable to keep my body still, I felt myself levitating toward X. Our eyes locked as they had in the car, drawn together.

"You can't be that stupid," I retaliated. "You suggesting I'm not black? On what basis?"

"Hell, no, you ain't black…not anymore! You used to be black," he screamed through an explosion of spittle and sweat. The muscles in his throat rippled.

A tingling sensation buzzed in my fingertips, and I could feel my peers and students watching me, gawking at the black sideshow.

"Oh, okay," I responded sarcastically. "So, you think you are somehow more black than I am? And what is the reason for that? What solidifies *your* blackness, X?"

X did not speak. He allowed his head to drop as if in a moment of reverie.

Ross stepped between us and placed his enormous hands on my chest. The weight of his palms pushed me backward. I stumbled a bit and tried to control the firestorm of rage pulsating in my brain. X's voice began to cut through the breeze. It sliced its way through the space between us. "I ain't scared to tell you why," he retorted after his brief contemplation. "You got your degrees and PhDs, and now you think you're better than the rest of us. I'm out here in the real world, man. The real world! This campus ain't the real world. Those books that you write and read ain't the real world either."

"What?" I interrupted. "I don't—"

Ross chimed in, "Bernard, let him finish! Let him get it out."

X continued, "Yeah, that's right. You spend your time paying attention to theories and models and all that other bullshit you read. That shit ain't real. I'm real. I'm a man. I don't mince words, and I don't walk around smiling every time one of these white people on campus acknowledges me. So what that they call you 'doctor?' Besides," he continued, "you never fight back. If I punched you in your face right now, you would just let me do it, wouldn't you? You wouldn't even fight back. What kinda black man don't fight back?"

"Whatever," I responded, trying to pretend his words didn't hurt, trying to conceal the pain of his attack, the shock of the moment.

X continued, "You want some more reasons! Okay, here's more. You married that white bitch. Why the hell would you go and do that? And you work with all these white people. You live in a white suburb. You got half-white kids. You don't even think like a black man."

A flash of red erupted in my mind. "Don't call my wife that," I retorted.

Ross spoke up, "That ain't' right, man. You are way out of line, X."

"Whatever," X responded. "That is what she is. That's what they all are."

I imagined myself slamming X to the ground, stomping on him over and over, crushing his skull into the brick and stone of the library wall. I had been in quite a few fights in my lifetime, and I longed to revisit those moments. Unable to stand the moment any longer, I turned on my heels and walked slowly toward my office. My shoes scraped the concrete as I hurried away, fists clenched. Despite being forty years old, my eyes began to fill with water. I hadn't cried since my eleven-year-old daughter was born. I fought with all of my might to restrain the deluge of childlike tears threatening to rush in like a desert sandstorm. In our entire lifetime together, X had never raised his voice to me. He had never lashed out at me. Our relationship had been peaceful, understanding—*brother's keepers*.

Refusing to turn around as I walked, I imagined X and Ross standing together under that enormous oak tree. I imagined the thin breeze blowing over them and saw the expressions etched into their faces—expressions of anger, of sadness, of disgust, of disbelief. As I entered my office, I sat at my desk and allowed the tears to fall. They came in gushing waves—a salty torrent. I kept checking the window of my office door to make sure there were no curious students milling about. I felt as if my center point had been removed and ripped out of my chest. And as I held my head in my hands and tried to catch my breath, I felt as if I'd lost a loved one, as if a soul had passed.

Moments later, however, the sadness began to morph into something very different. It began to roll over. It began to turn over on itself like an upset stomach. It quaked and churned until all that was left was rage. A visceral, primal rage that felt as if it were freezing at its base. I quickly reached down and opened my desk drawer to extract my laptop. It powered up immediately, and I opened it to a blank page and began to type. With haste—vigorously, wildly—I began to recount the day's events, every searing detail from the car trip to the public argument under the campus oak tree. I was writing to save myself—getting it out of me. My fingers banged the keys with fast and furious precision. It flowed out like running water. My tears slipped downward, creating a salty stream between my nose and upper lip. They fell into the cracks on the keyboard, yet I typed on, wiping my eyes between sentences.

As if I were dying, I typed and typed like my life depended on telling the story—therapeutic metacognition—pain on a wire.

And as I typed, I had an epiphany. I came to the realization that X was in competition with me—a competition of blackness. An unwinnable game in which he who does the right thing still loses. Right or wrong, in that game, "winning" was determined by one's ability to follow prescribed racial regulations. Black codes cultivated by black people about black people on black terms.

You see, my dear reader, all the things X had pointed out to me are, in fact, good things. Good things that should be celebrated and respected. But to X, they are antithetical to being authentically black. In his world, authentic blackness trumps all. It trumps love and marriage. It trumps social standing and spirituality. It trumps the love of a good woman. It trumps cultural development and educational prowess, peace, and maturity. It even trumps God.

Yes, I married a white woman. She is the most wonderful woman I have ever met—supportive and spiritual, soulful and intelligent. She has the heart of a saint. Growing up, I never imagined my wife would be white. It just happened, the way love so often does. We have been married for decades without a single incident of negativity or adultery, following God's plan. And although I realize she is white, I don't see her as white any longer. I see her as my life partner, the helpmate God placed here for me. Now it is true that the typical mythology germane to black and white marriages suggests that a black man finds a white woman after his success takes root. Perhaps after he makes his money or makes the team or makes partner, etc. This was hardly the case for me. When I met my wife, I had not achieved much from a professional, occupational, or academic perspective. I was down and out—no job, no goals, and living in the basement of friend's house. I had nothing and was going nowhere. She backed me up when others would not, and her support had nothing to do with her whiteness and everything to do with her soul. It had to do with who she was as a person—her character. And through her support, I was able to break out of my malaise and do something with my life. To move onward and upward.

To X, my wife's whiteness disqualifies her from being a decent person. To X, whiteness circumvents her saintliness. To X, whiteness limits her propensity to mother her children, love her husband, do well in her job, and follow her God. To X, whiteness ensures that she is, somehow, less of a human being, less of a woman, and that my marriage to her somehow confiscates my blackness, stealing it like a thief in the night. In X's mind, life is a contest of blackness, and the score is based on a twisted set of rules that limits one's ability to explore all that humanity has to offer. It is a contest, and according to him, he is winning the *Out-Black-Me* game, and the score is one to zero. But is he really?

My wife and I are blessed with three beautiful children—healthy, lively, precocious, and loveable kids. But because I am the father of three biracial children, X feels as if I am no longer black. He feels the whiteness flowing through the veins of my offspring obfuscates the realness of my children— the blackness of my children—thus stunting their racial growth. X feels that my kids have been tainted by the blood of the white man. That they are, somehow, less than they should be. So, he ignores their good grades, high test scores, impeccable manners, and respect for authority. He ignores their propensity to work hard and to respect their elders. To X, there is only one kind of black child—the one who lives as he lived and exists as he existed. To X, this is a game of blackness, and the score is two to zero. X is winning the *Out-Black-Me* game. But is he really?

After years of avoiding education, I fell in love with learning. As a result, I went to graduate school and never stopped. I was always apprehensive, but my wife encouraged me to continue. She reminded me that my life's narrative could be attractive to a classroom of students, and my ability to connect with people could circumvent barriers to that connectivity. Ten years later, I have earned several master's degrees, and I am working on a second PhD. Learning is who I am today. It is what drives me and shapes my worldview. Education has allowed me to become a college professor, a public speaker, and an international business consultant. It has allowed me to travel the world, develop systems of thinking, and touch lives. And while I am keenly aware my education will not protect me from institutionalized racism, it does provide my life with a purpose. However, according to X, my educational standing disqualifies me from being authentically black. To X, education is a game for the elite, and it forces a man to think in theories and ideals, principles and paradigms. To X, college is a white man's venture, and it should be enjoyed by white people. Never has he considered that education belongs to anyone who wishes to seek it. Never does he think about the fact that everything ever accomplished by the hands of man began as a theory, started as a paradigm, existed first as a principle. Never does he think that black people fought and died for the right to become educated, to obtain a college education, the right to read, and to express themselves, but to X, my PhD diminishes my blackness; it makes me less black, less real, and less true. It takes me outside of who I am supposed to be and places me into a category of whiteness. The score is three to zero, and in his mind, X is winning the *Out-Black-Me* game. But is he really?

My wife and I have always wanted to live in a place where we could have a safe and diverse environment for our children. We had prayed and worked hard to make this dream a reality. Our first apartment was in Westside Baltimore. Gunshots and murders were common occurrences. We vowed to make a better home and dreamed about it every night. We would lay in the bed at 3:00 a.m., talking about the way our home would look and imagining the details of our neighborhood. After saving our money for ten years, we purchased a house in the suburbs. We now have white, black, Asian, and African neighbors. Some are lawyers, others are doctors, teachers, and engineers—hardworking people. The kids exist within a wholesome environment and attend private schools, play soccer, and study piano—so many things I never did. Our kids are safe, and this allows me to sleep at night, to rest easy. But, according to X, living in the culturally mixed suburbs reduces the chances of my children being authentically black. He suggests, somehow, this robs them of their true calling—their true *black* calling. To X, piano and soccer and orchestra and multiculturalism are for white kids with freckles and blond hair. To X, black kids play basketball and football. They don't read. They don't play piano. They cuss and fight. They hurt one another and subscribe to a "crab in the barrel" ideology. The score is four to zero, and in his mind, X is winning the *Out-Black-Me* game. But is he really?

My wife and I are Christians. We attend church and follow the Bible as best we can. In the spirit of Ghandi and Dr. King, we have decided to raise our kids as pacifists. We respect the power of Satyagraha and nonviolence, the example of Jesus turning the other cheek. But we also teach our children that being human is a complex concept that often requires a bit of duality. There are times to fight and scream as well as times to remain silent and love. While we sometimes fail to accomplish such a lofty goal, the ideal of *love thine enemy*, is real to us. To X, however, pacifism is not what real black men do. He sees this ideology as a weakness. It is for this reason X ridiculed me for not fighting back, for not kicking and slapping and punching him during our altercation, for not screaming at him and spitting in his face. All the while, he is missing the point. *I am fighting back.* I am fighting back by being faithful to my wife, working hard, educating myself, setting lofty goals, and teaching my children the power of nonviolence and situational decision making. I am fighting back by helping Ross to build his résumé and setting X up to attend college. I am fighting back by building a coalition of friends and family who are white and black and Muslim and Korean and Latino and gay and straight and educated and not educated and so on. I am fighting back by teaching. I am fighting back by following God's plan and attending church, writing books, reading everything I can get my hands on, and setting an example for my kids. I am fighting back by being the best person I can be, the best black father I can be, the best black husband I can be, the best black college professor I can be . . . but in X's mind, the score is five to zero, and he has officially won the *Out-Black-Me* game. But has he really?

Chapter Four

You Love Who You Love, Race Notwithstanding

When I say I grew up black, I am not kidding. I was raised in an earth-toned patch of burgeoning blackness. The kind of blackness that seeps into your pores and smells of birch-burned incense and cocoa butter. I come from that profound intense blackness. Hold-one-fist-in-the-air blackness. I grew up surrounded by wooden furniture and African art. Ethiopian sculptures of long-faced women with extended lips and raised foreheads. Braided indoor wicker baskets filled with synthetic bamboo. Orange and yellow paintings of the female black form with arms outstretched, bronzed breast exposed to the light. We had random collections of Goli masks strewn across our paneled walls, and I recall the proverbial white shag carpet as well. Blackness was everywhere.

I can't remember a single day of my childhood without black music. But not the kind of black music that tends to exist on the Top 40 charts. The music in my house was permeated with substance. Music with a plot. It was soulful, mood bending music that slanted toward the most revolutionary of ideals. Nina Simone and Gill Scott Heron. John Lucian and Barkley Hendricks. Man, I heard Marvin Gaye's "What's Going On" so many times I thought it was the black national anthem. It was much later I learned that title belonged to James Weldon Johnson's "Lift Every Voice and Sing."

In addition to the art and music, every shelf in my childhood home held a book by a black author. Books were everywhere. They were laying on coffee tables and stacked under wooden lamps. I remember using them as a door stop when the dog kept coming into my room. Morrison and Walker. Angelou and Wright. Hell, the first book of any real substance I remember reading is Claude Brown's *Manchild in the Promised Land*. I was twelve. It knocked my socks off.

Chapter Four

My surroundings included more, however, than just black material things. My house was constantly filled with an elixir of black people. Aunts with swaying hips and too much makeup seemed to waltz through our front door daily. They would hug my mother, wrapping their skinny arms around her waist before plopping down on the orange sectional. Kicking off their shoes and exposing those long brown legs, they would summon me over and use their softened hands to reshape my afro. They'd kiss me on the cheek and tell me how beautiful my eyes were. Wiping the lipstick off my face, I would run to the door and peek out of the fingerprint-stained glass to see if my cousins were in the car. They would jump out of the olive-green Pinto or off-white Fiat and scamper into our diminutive townhouse with laughter and smiles. We would play marbles or jacks, but eventually we would head out into the tiny backyard to play freeze tag or tackle football.

The sounds inside that tiny house would expand like a filled lung. Satisfying the entirety of the kitchen and living rooms, those sounds of blackness would ebb and flow. Signifying giggles. Fingers and slapped hands. The sucking of teeth. My aunts' husbands or my dad's brothers would always enter around the back of the house. They would amble through the kitchen and ease their way down the steps to the box-shaped basement. I would sometimes dip down the steps and sit on the beanbags amongst the men. I liked their male aroma. They smelled of old leather and dried out marijuana. Their conversations ran the gamut but always seemed to take the form of a question. Socratic black talk from black men in the late '70s trying to survive. Trying to comprehend their place in that world.

When the hell is Jimmy Carter gonna fix this gas crises? How the hell am I supposed to get back and forth to work when the damn gas lines is five blocks long? My boss don't like black folk, and he can't wait to fire my ass.

Man, this government got all this money to spend on a damn test tube baby, but my paycheck ain't barely enough to stay ahead of my rent. Why they focusing more on that science shit than helping me take care of my family?

What y'all think about that Son of Sam? They done caught his ass now. Y'all think they gonna sentence him to as many years as they would if he was black?

Ever since I got back from Vietnam, I ain't been right, man. I get these dreams, man.

I can't stop shaking, and I ain't never hungry. What y'all think is wrong with me?

Woo-wee! Is that Jane Kennedy on the TV right there? I saw her the other day in that police woman movie. Man, she is fine as frog hair. Which one of y'all would give up your wife for one night with her?

Ever since they been bussing my kids to that white school over on the other side of town, my son been having a hell of a time. He keep getting into fights with those white boys. I told him to stay away from those white girls. Y'all think he gonna listen?

After playing outside, the kids would trample back into the house, clothes coated in grass and mud stains from the backyard. We would wash our hands single file and sit at the kids' table with watering mouths, preparing to eat. Black food. Soul food. Food that tastes good going down but causes a multitude of problems down the line. Heart disease. Obesity. High blood pressure. But damn, it hit the spot. Cornmeal or pan-fried fish. Collard greens and fried okra. Honey yams with air-puffed biscuits so big you could easily mistake them for softballs. Butter dripping between the flakes. Too much salt on everything and red Kool-Aid that stained our teeth when we smiled.

Yeah, when I say I grew up black, I am not kidding. To be honest, this is why it seems so strange to me I married a white woman. Even now, twenty years into a happy marriage, I remain surprised. Long ago, it had seemed as if all the spaces analogous to my existence were far removed from whiteness, especially white women. I mean, don't get me wrong, I had a few white friends and female teachers, and I oftentimes found myself lost in the aura of a few white television shows of that era. *The Partridge Family* and *Laverne and Shirley. Happy Days* was a favorite. But those shows and those teachers always appeared to dwell on the periphery. Never reaching my essence. Never establishing a visceral connection. Come to think of it, though, there were scattered remnants of whiteness in my childhood home that were deemed at least relatively acceptable. Flickers of whiteness that were given credence. But even those remnants seemed to be steeped in counterculture, which, in some way, made their presence seem tolerable. I remember, for example, my father's Janis Joplin album cover laying on the corner of his art table. I would stare it frequently. It was the 1971 *Pearl* album. The photo on the cover was mesmerizing. It was framed in violet plum with a deep blue inset. Joplin sat leaning on her side, with her fingers wrapped around what appeared to be a bottle of wine. Her dress hung to the floor. It was an oversized shade of blood red, and her sweater was dipped in varied pinks and fuchsias. I remember staring at the wildness of her hair. The way it protruded at various angles. Her hanging scarves and necklaces. The smile on her face was illuminating yet whimsical . . . like she was keeping a secret. Hardly a classical beauty, but there was something about her. Something that drew me to her. It could have been the child that seemed to live behind her young adult eyes. She had a kind of youthful exuberance. What the old folk today refer to as a wild streak. It was years later I learned who Joplin really was and the significance of her place in American history.

Although she died in 1970, presumably of a heroin overdose, that album cover photo of her is still very much alive in my mind.

Despite my fascination with the album cover, I was never consciously attracted to white women. For the most part, I gravitated to the little black girls in my class. I can remember my first girlfriend. Her name was Alice. We met on the first day of kindergarten. I can't remember our initial conversation, but I do remember I could not keep my eyes off her. She had a feline sense of familiarity. It was as if I knew her before I knew her. Her skin was a light honey brown, and her hair was thick and tightly curled. We would hold hands during recess, and I can remember laying on a plastic mat beside her during naptime. She would sleep, and I would watch her, gazing at the curve of her neck as it rested on the little pink pillow that she used during every naptime. I remember her smell because it was a similar smell to the women who so often occupied my house. Shea butter and Ultra Sheen. Alice became the prototype. My girlfriends and crushes in elementary school all seemed to display Alice-like characteristics. Hell, I even married an Alice-like archetype when I turned twenty-four. It only lasted three years. We were young and not really ready for marriage. It was like we were playing house, and outside of a rather potent sexual connection, our relationship was emotionally flimsy at best. But she was black, and up until that point, being with a black woman was, I thought, my destiny. That was until . . . well, until I met Heather.

Heather and I have been married for over twenty years. We have two girls, ages nineteen and twelve, and a fifteen-year-old son. She and I have seen every form of racism possible. I have been pulled over by police officers while she sat in the passenger seat, scared I might be dragged out and beaten to death. We have been ignored in restaurants by employees not interested in serving the biracial couple. We have stayed up late waiting for our son to get home from football practice, fearing he was stopped and held up by a bad cop. She has held my hand and cried with me while I explained to her I was fired from my job by a manager who displayed racist tendencies. I have held her hand and watched the anger in her face while she explained she was questioned by a random woman about the legitimacy of our child. We have had tough conversations about white privilege, sending our daughter to an historically black college, and how our marriage is so different than most other marriages. Through it all, however, it is clear to me that although I grew up black, Heather is my soulmate. She is the one God chose for me, and I would be an idiot to go against God. You love who you love. Race notwithstanding.

Chapter Five

The Truth about Blackness
Navigating Free Black Will

The truth about blackness: black people are not a monolith. We are many things, and we dwell in many places. Our thoughts run the gamut. The connection between black people is omnipresent. It sticks to the souls of us. It pulls us together. Fusing us. Mending us into a potlatch of pliable limbs and beating hearts. Blackness is a duality. In one respect, it is an alloy, a combined cross section of similar elements pressed together to create something ethically distinct in nature. In another respect, it is a bifurcated segmentation of agreed upon sociocultural and ethnic commonalties.

Despite our connectivity, blackness does seek, at times, to differentiate itself. It is for this reason that, when I see a brother with eyes and lips like my own, I tend to revel in the aesthetic sameness before me. I recognize that link, that oneness. But it is vital I take a broader vantage point so I do not let that which lives on the exterior fool me into thinking he and I are the same. We are not. Nor should we try to be. Yes, he and I are brothers, but even twins are granted souls and spirits of their own. Yes, he is my brother, and I love him. I understand his plight. I feel the interlocked drumbeats of history, the whispered chants of our ancestors. I know he hears it as well. But I also realize he and I have been awarded a special gift. A gift mired in our humanity, the gift of free will—*free black will.*

It is that freeness, so to speak, which allows black men and women to demonstrate their own ideas regarding love, life, sexuality, war, politics, religion, art, death, fear, pain, pleasure, and so on. Free black will gives black folks the power to select and defend their own political, social, and spiritual ideologies. To cultivate their own socio-ethical philosophies and develop their own psychocultural rules of thumb—free black will. It affords black people the freedom to be what they want to be; to marry whomever they want to marry; to think however they want to think; to follow the God they wish to follow;

to fight under whatever flag they choose; to just *be*. These distinctions do not weaken the bond between black people. They do not sever the alloy. Rather, these distinctions allow black people to express their individuality. To be black in America is to be many things. It is both personal and communal. Black people are here and there. They are up and down, right and left, always loving, always expanding . . . and always negotiating the jagged labyrinth of free black will.

Chapter Six

Ink Black and Rail Thin

I parked the car and grabbed my bag. It was full of graded papers and final exams. I shut the car door and quickly progressed toward my classroom. I arrived, and there he was, blocking the door. I slowed my pace and took a deep breath. A few seconds later we were face to face. I said hello. He squinted his eyes and lifted his left hand toward my face. He pointed and shook his index finger. He reminded me he was the department chair of the business school. I rubbed my forehead and explained I was fully aware of his title. He winced at my tone. I tried to slide past him so I could enter my class. He blocked me again. He told me my class was scheduled to begin at 9:00 a.m. I checked my watch. It said 8:58 a.m. He saw me checking my watch and moved closer to my face. I smelled the coffee on his breath. I was a few inches taller than him. I looked down into his eyes. The whiteness of his skin reflected from the class window. I asked him to move. He raised his voice and explained I should arrive at my classes at least ten minutes before the scheduled start time. I again rubbed my face and politely asked him if he would let me enter the class. He said if it happened again, I would need to teach Business 101 somewhere else. I reminded him I was voted professor of the year by the students. I reminded him I was the only current faculty member with five master's degrees and a PhD. I reminded him I had never been officially late, and I had never heard of his new "arrive ten minutes early rule." He unblocked the door. I walked past him. I saw my students. They appeared to be embarrassed for me. I placed my bag on the desk and walked over to the lectern. My anger was visible. I paused. A student stood up. She was ink black and thin as a rail. She walked toward the front of the class and headed to the door where the self-identified department chair of the business school was standing. She asked him to back up a few feet. He was confused, but took a few steps backward. He smiled nervously. She closed the classroom door in his face and walked back to her seat. The students erupted in laughter. He smirked through the window of the classroom door and gave me that look. That look white men like to give. The one that said he had the power. And I realized, instantly, that would be my last class at that university. I realized, instantly, that when my class was over, I would be summoned to his office, and I would be told I was fired. And I realized, instantly, I didn't have tenure, and no matter how angry I was . . . he *had* the power. The power to take me away from my students and my love of teaching and my desire to enlighten those who wished to learn. He walked away. My eyes transferred to the ink black, rail-thin student. She smiled and asked, "So which chapter are we covering today?"

Chapter Seven

Dubois Talks about That Twoness

Dubois talks about that twoness
That struggle to be in two black spaces at the same black time
That struggle to walk that white line
While remaining in line with that dark tone in your face
That struggle for twoness leaves me exhausted
Sucking air and holding my chest
Trying to catch my breath for both of my selves
That self that likes to tilt my head to the side and pull the brim of my cap over my eyes
And
That self that smiles and wears a tie and tucks in my shirt playacting for that paycheck
Struggling
Struggling
Struggling to maintain both sides of that twoness
And
Remaining black all the while.

Chapter Eight

Lessons of a Mixed-Race Family
You Can't Have It Both Ways

It was a Saturday morning in Maryland. The winter sky was impregnated with clouds, and the sun bit through the cold as if it had teeth. My wife eased the minivan into the IHOP parking lot. All three kids jumped out, slammed their doors, and the five of us ambled into the restaurant. Within seconds, we were seated. When the waitress came to our table, our three-year-old asked for pancakes with bacon. Our six- and ten-year-olds selected waffles and eggs. My wife and I ordered omelets and juice.

As is always the case when one takes children out to breakfast, nature tends to call. My wife remarked it was her turn to lead the troops. She rose from her seat, took a sip of her orange juice, and escorted the three- and ten-year-olds to the bathroom. I watched her walk away and admired the soft roll of her hips as she and the kids disappeared into the women's bathroom. I looked at my son sitting to my left. I allowed my eyes to travel over the corkscrew curls and crimped follicles exploding from the roundness of his scalp. Shiny and black, his hair was shaped into a tumescent afro. Faded on the sides, it gave way to a premature illusion of eventual sideburns. It was a prelude to manhood. His skin looked like warm clay—supple and light brown.

As he sat there, drawing basketballs on his napkin and humming under his breath, I was overwhelmed by the way he looked at that moment. The beauty that dwelled within him. He was a racial mishmash of black and white, cultivated from the power of an interracial love affair.

You see, dear reader, I am black—silent-moments black; onyx black; deep, obsidian, inky black; the kind of black reminiscent of midnight or outer space. My blackness and I share the same space.

On the other hand, my wife is white. She is a soft, achromatic, milky white. Her skin is pallid and smooth to the touch. She is the kind of white that allows one to see every freckle. To see the blue veins pulsating under the skin along with the tiny, blonde strings of hair on her arms. Our son, Isaiah, is a mixture of both of us. He is our most wonderful elixir, and what amazes me about him is the way he seems to transmute based on the light and location of the current moment. The way he morphs into people of a distant land while barely moving. You see, Isaiah—depending on the angle—sometimes looks Mediterranean. When the light hits his face, he can pass for a meandering child of Malta or Montenegro. Yet, in an instant, he can turn his head and appear to be Palestinian or Sudanese, maybe even Cuban. On other days, he could pass for Tutankhamun or a childhood Ramses. His appearance runs the gamut.

As I watched him sitting there, showing off the abnormal largeness of his eyes, I wondered if he cared about his propensity to radiate a collection of disparate ethnicities. I wondered if he cared about the German and Saharan blood coursing within him, flowing like a genetic rivulet throughout his entire body. I wondered if he cared about his future as a black man with a white momma. I watched him closely, staying in tune with the rise and fall of his breath, the brown in his cheeks. I loved him dearly. He couldn't have seemed to care less, so I let the thought evaporate, pushing it well beyond my current state of mind. Somewhere into the stratosphere. I focused more on the smell of bacon and coffee circulating from the IHOP kitchen. The clanging of pots and pans. The murmur of the countless meals in process.

Recognizing that Isaiah was beginning to get a bit antsy, I leaned over the table and placed my hand on his arm. Our pulses beat in unison.

"Are you good?" I asked him. He smiled back at me, teasing me with his dimples and thick eyelashes.

"Yeah, Daddy, I'm fine."

As I leaned back in my chair and sipped the pulp from my orange juice, I watched three men being escorted by the waitress. They headed toward the table located directly behind Isaiah and me. I pushed my chair in so they could pass. They smelled of cologne and aftershave. Each of the men was black, one a bit darker than the others, one a bit larger than the others. They were dressed in jeans, golf shirts, and leather jackets. They looked to be in their late forties, but it was difficult to tell. As they walked by, our eyes met. I nodded hello with a straight face and tight lips, lifting my chin toward the ceiling—the universal sign among men with skin like mine. Soul brothers. The men smiled in approval and nodded back, connection established. One of them winked at Isaiah and gave him a thumbs-up. Isaiah smiled back nervously and continued to draw on his napkin. He kicked the base of his chair a bit too loudly, so I placed my hands on his knee and told him to chill out. Isaiah kept his eyes on his artwork, and his feet remained still.

I could almost read the men's thoughts as they sat in their seats, still smiling at my son and me, taking pride in my choice to be there with him, next to him, part of him.

One of the men spoke up as he readjusted himself in his chair. "God bless you, brotha. It's always nice to see a black man spending time with his son. You are doin' a good thing. We need more black fathers to step up." I nodded in response and took another sip of my juice.

Eventually, the men ordered coffee and began a conversation regarding the church to which they belonged. Evidently, they had just left a church meeting. I struggled to hear, so I eased my chair over a bit. The darkest man, the one with large hands and bald head, led the discussion. He tapped his feet as he spoke. With a voice like gravel, the man pointed out on several occasions that the primary role of the church should be to help black men, to reach out to brothers who needed support—Black Liberation Theology. The other men nodded in agreement and chimed in at varied intervals. They reiterated God had a plan that included upward mobility for black men, and the church should ensure black men were respected, especially those black men who were serving as the heads of their families, strong Christian families, families that needed to be uplifted and respected for following God's plan.

One of the men pointed to me and Isaiah to make his point. "Just like this young brother over here. This brother is spending time with his son, and we should support that. Most black problems are generational, and they start with the absence of the father," the man said.

I listened intently as they spoke, and in many respects, I agreed with their general ideology. I even thought to myself, *I might want to join such a church. I, too, care about the needs of black men and the futures of little black boys. I, too, want to support black men and be supported as a black father.*

The smaller man began highlighting the need to cultivate and support future black leaders . . . maybe even presidents. Future Obamas. "If we can elect a man we love and admire who is also black," said the man, "then we need to figure out a way to help other black men do the same. I love my president," he proudly exclaimed. "And I don't care who is mad about that. But we gotta use the church to help these black boys grow into men like Obama, men who can be something of importance, men who can change the world."

As a fan of President Obama, my heart began to swell. I finished the last of my juice and wondered when my wife and girls would return from the bathroom. I was sure she would approve of these men. She would respect their points of view, for she and I were aligned politically as well as spiritually. God was a big deal in our house.

Within seconds, my wife returned to the table. The sunlight cracked through the window and bounced beautifully off the hazel in her eyes. She smiled and helped the kids back into their seats. They settled in. The ten-year-old turned on her iPod and stared out the window. I smiled at her preteen disinterest.

It felt as if the men at the table behind us were watching me. I could feel the heat from their eyes. It burned the back of my neck. As I turned around, the larger man turned down the corners of his lips, his face contorted as if he had tasted something sour. His pupils seemed to radiate.

"Are you serious?" he exclaimed, loud enough for us to hear. Gruffness grew in his voice, loud enough for the entire restaurant to hear. "That is a shame. I guess he could not find a black woman to marry. Had to get a white girl, huh?"

My fingers clutched the table, and I could feel muscles in my neck tightening. I started to turn around, but my wife placed her hand on my arm. Her touch cooled the fire in my spirit, but I could not hold back the waterfall of rage . . . fury . . . all of the questions that poured into my mind, filling up the spaces between my thoughts. So many questions. I wanted to stand up, turn around, and hurl a myriad of queries at the so-called men of God.

Are you going to sit here in front of my family and disrespect what God has done for us, the way He has brought us together, the way He has crafted and woven our love into a secure family unit? Ours is functional and loving . . . and, by the way, I thought you were Christians. Are you Christians? Does your Christianity promote or demote based on race? Does it support the venom spewing from your lips? Is that in your Bible? If so, what page is it on, 'cause I wanna read it, brotha . . . I wanna see it with my own eyes.

I thought you wanted to help black men. Isn't that what you said earlier, when you first sat down? Or were you only referring to black men who are married to black women . . . black men who follow your rules? What about the black men who fall in love with Asian women or Latino women or Greek women? Does my blackness become less significant in the eyes of God because of whom I marry?

What about my baby girls? Aren't they black women? Do they deserve to hear you speaking that way about their mother? And when they hear you speaking that way about their mother today in this restaurant, does it secure a positive image in their minds about black men? Is that how God wants you to speak? Do you speak to your kids like that? What if I spoke that way about your mother? What would you do?

What about my son? Is he less black as well? Is he less important than when you first saw him and winked at him a few moments ago? And what about your statement about black men and the president? How can you love the president and not love the union between my wife and me? Do you realize that the president is my son? That my son is the president? That the president shares the same interracial makeup, the same skin of soft clay and curly hair, the same white mother and black father . . . deep, inky black and soft, achromatic white.

And what about all those black leaders, writers, and actors? Thinkers who were birthed from white mothers? Do you respect them? Do you respect Fredrick Douglass and Nella Larsen, Walter Mosley and Langston Hughes, Bob Marley and Maya Rudolph? Booker T. Washington, Ben Jealous, James McBride, August Wilson, Sade, Zadie Smith, Malcolm Gladwell, Mario Van Peebles, Eartha Kitt, Giancarlo Esposito, Gina Belafonte. Which side of the president do you love more? How can you seek to have it both ways, brother? Don't you get it? No black and white union, no Barack Obama.

You can't have it both ways brotha. You can't have it both ways!

Chapter Nine

For Those Who Overlook What Really Happened

Imagine
Genuflecting imagery of stalking thieves
stealing your chief in the African night heat . . .
bonding his heated flesh
with nets and wired mesh
while he screams nightmarish dreams to be free
Imagine
That pulsating lump in his throat
when he was tossed on that boat
shackled
Twisting in his own urine and feces
Coughing up pieces of phlegm
His body sapped and overlapped by those breaking down
Frayed decay
Imagine
Slipping in and out of consciousness
Moaning with segmented narratives untold
Below sea deck . . .
Screaming through nightmarish
Dreams to be Free

Chapter Ten

Racial Reality Intelligence
The Truth Will Set America Free

There are obvious correlations between the concepts of truth and reality, especially as they relate to ideas concerning race in America. To claim truth and reality are constructs that bleed into one another is an understatement. When something is considered to be true, we are suggesting it is a fact or a reality. On the other hand, when we say something is grounded in reality, we are suggesting it is based in truth. Both ideas dwell within the open spaces of our individual minds but also live in the physiosocial world that surrounds us. The constructs are connected at the hip. Through closer examination, however, we recognize where a fissure appears. We uncover the complex dimension in which we see the separation between what I tend to think of as *my black truth* and *my black reality*. Let us begin by examining the former.

My *black truth* has to do with the way I am perceived by many white people. The way my blackness requires walking through a sociological minefield replete with a set of Americanized capitalistic heuristics. You see, my black truth can arise when I choose to raise my voice in public. It is the way my raised tone is so readily associated with black physicality. Rules that dictate that black anger is bloodthirsty and animalistic. That it manifests itself in the forms of violence and crime and barbarism. So, when I am little loud, I'm no longer considered human. When I am loud, I am poised to strike.

Although I have never committed a crime, my black truth seems to lead to being followed into dressing rooms and accused of stealing pants. It leads to being thrown onto hoods of cars by police officers, fired from jobs, passed over for promotions, underpaid, and disrespected—all because my smile sometimes turns to a smirk. But my smirk is a black smirk, so apparently, it's loaded. My black truth hinges on the fact that I am hunted at night by police officers seeking to rid me of this planet. Seeking to separate me from my wife and children. Seeking to place me within the monstrous jaws of the prison industrial complex. My black truth is intermingled with a wealth of statistical data that suggests I will be sent to jail for a crime I did not commit, sent to trial with inept public counsel, or sent to die slowly from heart disease, COVID-19, malignant neoplasms, stroke, diabetes, kidney disease . . . my black truth is deadly.

Reality, as a construct, is subject to interpretation, meaning that because of our ethical, social, and cultural differences, we may experience disparate understandings of reality. We do not necessarily reach upward for reality; reality is not always lofty. It tends, instead, to be at eye level—right in front of our faces—which brings us to *my black reality*. The most pressing and frustrating aspect of my black reality is that, no matter how hard I try to avoid my black truths, I will never outmaneuver the pain of my racial circumstances. I cannot outgrow it. I cannot out work it or out educate it. I am stuck with it.

My black reality reminds me every day I will ultimately reach that moment when a white police officer will rest his knee on the back of my neck for eight minutes and forty-six seconds. . . until my breath eventually gives way to nothingness. *George Floyd.* That moment when six inner-city officers will beat me to death in the back of a moving police cruiser. *Freddie Gray.* That I will be shot to death in my vehicle on a routine traffic stop. *Sam DuBose. Philando Castile.* That I will be shot to death by an officer on the pavement outside of a convenience store. *Alton Sterling.* That I will be the next to be killed. *Jamar Clark. Jeremy McDole. Walter Scott. Eric Harris. Tamir Rice. Walter Brown. Eric Garner* . . . Bernard Grenway?

When we associate both ideas with the modern world, we begin to see that America has an obvious problem highlighting what is historically real. America has a problem with its propensity to demonstrate what I like to refer to as *racial reality intelligence*. So how does the duality of black truth and black reality relate to race in America? To answer that question, dear reader, we need to begin with a discussion regarding the concept of *intelligence*.

Now, it is true we could spend a great deal of time delving into the academic and theoretical controversies concerning the construct of intelligence. This would be an arduous task, however. I say this primarily because social scientists and psychologists have never agreed as to what constitutes intelligence. The argument has been sustained for generations, and circumventing the reams of literature on the subject saves us the work of drumming up models constructed by Howard Gardner, Alfred Binet, David Wechsler, Carl Rogers, and Alfred Adler. A discussion focusing on intelligence could span to kinesthetic, naturalistic, logical-mathematical, or intrapersonal frameworks. In most cases, however, intelligence is typically defined as the capacity to learn. Other definitions suggest intelligence has to do with the ability to acquire and/or apply knowledge.

To date, there have been innumerable studies focusing on emotional, cultural, environmental, social, and various other types of intelligence. All have added to the collective body of knowledge. Despite this, we need a more systematic and scientific methodology when it comes to determining how we think about the intersection between race and intelligence. It is important to note I am not referring to the differences between the intelligence of one race versus another. I am speaking instead about our capacity as a society to learn about our racial worlds. Is there such a thing as a racial truth? What about racial reality? Only when we take an active approach to uprooting historical falsehoods will we come to grips with who we truly are as Americans, as human beings. So, I introduce the theory of racial reality intelligence.

Racial reality intelligence focuses on the capacity to understand what is true and real regarding race in America. Individuals with high levels of racial reality intelligence demonstrate the unique ability to think abstractly about race (meaning they understand race is learned, race is not a biological fact, and race is used as a sociopolitical tool to classify and categorize American citizens). Racial reality intelligence highlights an individual's ability to effectively discern and define the parameters of their race and to do so based on socio-scientific points of reference. More importantly, it focuses on one's propensity to acquire racial knowledge (very much in line with cultural intelligence) and apply that knowledge in such a way that it serves as social benefit to disparate racial groups. Racial reality intelligence is an action-based theory. It seeks movement. Progress. It suggests once we develop a salient understanding of what it means to be black in America, we take active steps to help black folks find solace, support, and the means to be *free* in America.

Individuals with high levels of racial reality intelligence understand the role of black people has been overlooked regarding the forming and structuring of the nation, and the less that is known about the psychosocial realities of black life, the worse off the nation is. Racial reality intelligence seeks to promote those who respect the truth about America's racial problems and racial triumphs. The truth matters. The truth is both obstinate and unyielding. It cannot be stamped out. Truth rises to the surface of the American soil like a ragged patch of old pigweed, waiting to be admired or trampled. But it is always there. Nothing drives a man's soul like the truth. So, to possess racial reality intelligence is not only to seek the truth regarding blackness and whiteness in America but also to point out the truth, even when it goes against the status quo, even when it goes against what one has been taught—no matter what.

> I promote the historical truths surrounding Thomas Jefferson's sexual relationship with his slave, Sally Hemings, on the plantation of Monticello.

I promote the historical truths associated with George Washington's decade-long search for his runaway slave, Oney Judge, on the plantation of Mt. Vernon.

I promote the historical truths associated with the understudied and underreported life of A.G. Gaston—black multimillionaire business mogul of the early 1960s.

I promote the historical truths about Henrietta Lacks, whose cancer cells were taken from her dead corpse without her permission (or family's consent) and used to save millions of lives.

I promote the historical truth that the Oklahoma City bombing paled in comparison to the Tulsa race riots of 1921.

I promote the historical truth that the American slave trade was actually a global affair. Of the thirteen million slaves shipped in the Atlantic slave trade, only four hundred thousand were shipped to U.S. shores.

I promote . . . the truth!

Chapter Eleven

That Ceremonial Covering That is Me

Draped in that ceremonial coverage that is me,
I am all decked out.
Everyday . . .
I move about, nomadic, in a world permeated with monsters,
Horned animal beasts ambling awkwardly toward me.
They come from disparate angles . . . dressed in suits and ties
Dressed in blue uniforms with silver badges
With humps on their collective backs,
The Zombie Zeitgeist,
Attempting to take my happiness away
And yet I push on . . .
Slow motion and decorated in my full black man regalia,
Steadfast on that journey to put food in my babies' bellies
But this world is a cold place.
It freezes hot to the touch.
It singes a blistering white heat and bleeds a rivulet of bubbling crimson.
This world . . .
It's a cold place
Attempting to take my happiness away.
But I keep on . . .
Slow motion, trudging,
All decked out in my full black man regalia.

Chapter Twelve

Afroprovidential Redirection
That Force That Steps into the Gap

The air was cool in my office. Student midterms were recklessly strewn across my desk, some ruthlessly corrected and others alluringly void of red ink. Taking a deep breath, I rolled back on the wheels of my chair and stretched my arms contemplatively toward the ceiling. I slumped over the untidy paperwork and rubbed my hands across my bearded face. I was exhausted. While I couldn't see each thick bristle lining the contours of my unshorn chin, I could feel the grayness creeping clandestinely into each bristling follicle, pilfering what little youth I had left, stealing my time. My stomach felt heavy and fattish stuffed into my wrinkled dress pants as I grew older by the second.

Shaking my head, I allowed myself a few minutes away from the stack of uncorrected student dreams, and my eyes surveyed that room in which I had spent so much of my time. That room, where students gaggled like wild geese to tell sob stories as to why their final exam would be late or to plead for a letter of recommendation for a job that remained in the proverbial balance. That room, where I secretly worked on this book between Introduction to Marketing at noon and Conflict Resolution at three. That room I loved so much.

In the corner of the office, there were six medium-sized bookshelves buckling under the weight of works by Drucker, Maslow, Weber, Peters, and Kotter. A small radio lived squeezed between next semester's text for Introduction to Management Theory and an abstract sculpture I had hijacked from my mother's garage. Soft jazz pulsated from a minuscule speaker tucked between the books, thus increasing my desire to daydream, to rest again. I enjoyed the phlegmatic ride, coasting on the quiet velvetiness of Thelonious Monk, even for a moment—drifting. The walls of my office were covered with pictures of my children, their caramel skin and curly Hawaiian-like hair glistening from the reflection of the photoflash, the whiteness of their teeth . . . the gleam . . . the brightness prompted me to smile and frown at the same time as they seemed so far away from my present position. The adjacent wall ogled back at me like a prideful shrine of hubris and unadulterated didactic narcissism, mocking me. It showcased my diplomas plastered in the light and pressed inside a series of fingerprint-smudged, mismatched frames. They were all there, watching me as I worked, judging my moral fiber and judging the black academic intellectual I had so rapidly become as if to ask: *Who do you think you are? Who do you think you are?*

I was no longer a baby born into the world by way of Southeast D.C. No longer a toddler existing in a small townhouse in Columbia, Maryland, playing little league baseball with a collection of pale-faced suburban lawyers' kids. I was no longer a teenager living with my father's mother in inner-city Baltimore, where the sirens and screaming neighbors annoyed my mother, where gunshots blasted in the darkness. I could no longer smell sweat and Pet Milk creeping up the stairs into my widened nostrils. I was no longer a high school senior trekking to school and falling asleep on the subway headed for the corner of North Capital and Taylor streets on the northeast side of the city. I was no longer any of those things, but always all of those things. A human composite shaped by the various environments I had endured. Yet still there.

Still breathing.
Breathing still.

Each degree placed on that wall was watching me, mocking me as I pretended to grow up and become a part of the system. A testament of my psychological desire to overcompensate—to prove the world wrong, to overcome the realities germane to blackness, maleness, and life as I knew it. Those of us who were confronted with our skin color before our tiny brains were equipped to cope with who we were—where did we stand?

The bachelor's degree from the University of Maine that hung on the wall was a piece of decaying parchment that disguised the actual culture shock of being eighteen and living in a state with less than two percent black people. Just a piece of paper in a plastic frame. The graduate certificate from Cornell reminded me of my pompous addiction to tasting the sweet blandness of Ivy, to feel the acceptance. All three master's degrees on that wall; the PhD on that wall; documents that allowed me to do what I love, to teach . . . all trapped in that room I adored so much, gazing down at me from across my desk, judging me and qualifying me simultaneously—putting me in my place.

Looking past the clutter, I drifted away, descending into the subterranean folds of an immaculate reflection, wondering how all of it came to be—so much so fast. How I landed that gig and was the only African-American professor on that small suburban campus, trapped between the neighborhood pool and a health food store. How my former distaste for academic diligence completely shifted as I aged, transformed my life's journey, and provided me with a new craft—constant erudition—the ceaseless hunt for truth. How I came to get paid to stand in front of a sea of white, youthful faces and represent what almost did not exist: a black professor in rural Maryland, shining darkly. Turning that question on its sprawling back, I gradually began to remember the numerous close calls, the flashes of grace whereby my youthful life dangled like strange fruit from heaven's ceiling. Those moments when a fine line separated me from the college office in which I sat and the many other places where black male potential so often rested its lethargic carcass. It made one think of the numerous predicaments awaiting black and brown adolescent males, waiting to strike and teeming with bloodthirst. There were so many ways to be derailed.

Black youth in America are hunted throughout the night and mocked throughout the day. The black male, in all his blackness, is categorized by those who barely understand him. His rebellions are misunderstood, his anger is misdiagnosed, his sexuality is animalized, his intelligence is misinterpreted, and his survival is limited. Yet on occasion, black and brown boys are protected despite their naïve transgressions or economic circumstances. Some are spared. It is as if some metaphysical supremacy steps into the fold with divine intentions and outmaneuvers destiny, saving the black male child from himself. Saving him from:

the streets,
the prisons,
gang life,
the war overseas,
the grave,
sexual overcompensation,
STDs,
the pregnant teen girlfriend,
hypertension,
the sickle cell,
the early death,
the crack pipe,
malt liquor,
unaesthetic anesthetics,
the angry cop,
the racist teacher,
low self-esteem,
the enormous pain of existing where he is a stereotype and an archetype,
the self-hatred.

All of this was trapped in my moment's musings that day, and while it is true that some black male youth triumph over the statistics, there is no explicit terminology that confers legitimacy to these metaphysical miracles. There is no sociological phraseology or prescribed academic idiom defining the action that occurs when these young souls are liberated from their collective environments. This is highly problematic in that it overlooks a young man's accomplishments and suggests, at least superficially, that his success is both arbitrary and of little consequence or, even worse, that his success can be completely attributed to himself. That he, somehow, fell haphazardly into success or that he somehow became successful all on his own, that he is an island, that he slipped through the cracks, that those degrees on his wall are there because of him, and only him. To reduce both accounts is to oversimplify what being black is all about. What about the life force that stands above his decision to work hard or do nothing? What about the life force that is overtly recognizable but impossible to quantify? There must be a literary anecdote that illuminates the child who conquers his territorial demons and gives credit to the life force that cleared the way. The anecdote must not be overgeneralized but instead cater to the visceral narratives so often encountered by young people of color. In an attempt to provide an official theoretical structure for moments such as these, I put forward a series of contextual constructs entitled *Afroprovidential and Afraprovidential redirection*. The former refers to black boys, while the latter refers to black girls. Afroprovidential redirection transpires when a deity-like phenomenon amends the once prescribed sociological conditions for black and brown boys despite their desire to make deleterious decisions or exist in a world dead set on their very destruction. This concept stands as the literary antithesis regarding the multitude of false perceptions perpetuating negative images of black and brown boys. It questions the notion that young minorities, principally males, possess souls preordained to prison, crime, and so on. It contests counterfeit personifications so often popularized by both black and white culture and reiterates that no one group of people is ever just one thing. And so, every twenty-something black male with saggy jeans and a baseball cap is not gang affiliated—a preposterous premise. There are dark-skinned black males born in the city, living with a single parent who will overcome their circumstances. They will thrive in school, demonstrate respect for elders, shun gang life, love their mothers, never use drugs, and give back to the world community. Some will write books, teach college classes, obtain doctorates, raise their children, and go to church.

But even in these brief moments when youth and environment collide, smashing into one another, leaving fragments of potential and intellect in tiny pieces on a city street, a life force will step into the gap. The circumstances will be interrupted by a moment of grace designed specifically for the least of these, designed for young people of color, created specifically for black men—for he who needs it most. It is for that moment I have coined Afroprovidential redirection. *Afro* refers to the specific cultural disparities pertaining to black male youth. *Providential* is derived from the root word "providence," which means luck, shedding light on the second chance provided for these children. When this unfolds, as the term dictates, the individual is spiritually and socially redirected—put back on track, if you will. It reminds us that even those who are an endangered species are loved by a higher power. It is Afroprovidential cultural grace that actually redirects the life of the black male child and alters his very destiny. In looking at my life, there are more than a few of these moments. One such moment occurred some twenty-five years ago. I lived with my roommate and school friend Lorenz on the west side of Baltimore.

It was a customary Friday night, one on which the tiny two-bedroom residence was overflowing with co-ed twenty-somethings frantically in search of unchaperoned adrenaline. Wu-Tang Clan's gruff inflections pulsated from the oversized speakers buttressed on the dilapidated kitchen counter, while naive bodies danced and sipped cheap wine from paper cups. The base shook the drywall while the foot traffic quadrupled with haste. The living room reeked of youthful sweat and balmy perfume. The girls swung their hips and purses as they performed like stunningly bizarre birds struggling to attract a mate with powerful wings, the kind of wings that could lift their skinny, tanned, feline torsos completely off the ground—wings of gossamer, wings I doubted I had. Watching my intoxicated peers, I slowly realized I was the only sober person in the room, yet I pretended to be drunk with the hope it made me look mature. An unexpected knock rattled the apartment door, barely audible through the breaks in the music. Since the general rule was to come in without knocking first, I wondered who it could be. I lifted myself from the couch, swayed through the dancing masses, and peeped through the eyehole. Gawking back through the hole, I could see our neighbor—his gray, ruffled eyebrows angrily furrowed into his forehead.

I winced as he stood stiffly, his arms crossed over what was probably at one time a taut abdomen but was just a reminder of his impotence in the face of anticipated disrespect.

"What?" I yelled over the music, trying to sound as mature as possible.

The man's lips tightened as he spoke. "Y'all gonna have to turn that damn music down. I can't hear myself think," he retorted.

Despite my healthy respect of karma and a gnawing instinct to revere my elders, assuredly implanted by my parents, I again pressed my eye to the peephole and screamed over the music, "Go away, man. We ain't turning nothing down. Get the hell outta here!"

As the words sprang from the back of my throat, a wave of embarrassment washed over me, an emotional wave that originated at the top of my skull and burned its way to the underside of my feet, reminding me of the boorish impudence of my behavior. Disrespecting that man, who resembled my father and grandfather, brought that strong feeling of nausea just prior to vomiting. Yet I felt empowered by the moment, shored up by the music, and supported by the ethnically conjoined souls cramped in that minuscule apartment. Not waiting for a response, I swaggered back through the room, resumed my seat on the couch, and got lost in the sanctuary of what I did not care to know. I did not care to know what the man's reaction must have been to hearing that insolent pre-adult speak to him as if he was some obtuse bother living across the corridor. I did not wish to know that the man thumped his fist on that door in livid aggravation and shambled, on his war-torn leg, across the hall to his tiny space. I did not wish to know that the man had rancorously quarreled with his much younger wife, who scolded him for bothering the kids next door who were just trying to have a little fun. I did not wish to know that the man picked up his phone and called the police, and so I reveled in my ignorance.

Hearing a second knock, I again arose from the couch and headed for the door. A girl I had never seen before with skeletal features and too much lipstick stretched her lanky arms toward the knob. I stopped her.

"Don't open it. I got this. It's just the guy from across the hall again. I'll deal with it." The girl's feline eyes met mine, and I could smell the Boone's Farm oozing from the warm pores of her skin.

"Can you do me favor before you get that?" she asked, leaning her mouth toward my ear.

"Yeah," I replied.

Her lean fingers, long and bony, dug into her cheap plastic purse and retrieved a clear zip lock bag stuffed with marijuana. A large bag. A bag big enough to send someone to jail for a while, big enough to get someone in trouble, stuffed to capacity. My eyes dropped. The pounding on the door seemed to escalate in cantankerous force and irritating consistency.

"Oh, nah, girl. I don't do that. That's not my thing," I explained. The girl rolled her eyes and ran her hand through the tracks in her hair.

She spit her gum on the floor and seemed to clear her thoughts. "I don't want you to smoke it, stupid. I just need you to hold it for me for a second."

"What the hell for?" I asked. "That's a big-ass bag."

Still playing with her store purchased locks, she shifted her weight and scratched the bottom of her chin. "I took it out of my girlfriend's purse, and

I want to see her face when she can't find it. We just messin' with her, you know. This is worth a lot of money, and she is gonna trip when she sees it gone. We just playin' with her. Here, just hold it for a second."

I could hear the pounding on the door, amplified by what sounded like several fists, feet, and bodies all banging in unison. Rushed by the reality of the moment, I sucked my teeth, grabbed the bag, stuffed it into the back pocket of my oversized jeans, and reached to open the door. As my hands felt the coolness of the knob, the door rocked off its hinges, catching me in the forehead and knocking me to the ground. Vision blurry, my equilibrium was confiscated for a moment. I fell back against the wall, knocking over a cheap painting, scrambling to get on my feet. My eyes widened while four of Baltimore's finest stepped coolly into the room. Each one, their skin as white as cotton tees, surveyed the surroundings. The music stopped. The dancing stopped. The drinking stopped. My heart began to stop. Somehow, I managed to get to my feet. For an instant, no one spoke. The room sat there, inside of itself, drenched in discomfort.

His breath brazened with gin and orange juice, Lorenz approached the officer. Wiping the perspiration from his face he asked, "What's the problem, sir?"

The officer chuckled under his breath and stepped closer to Lorenz. "I want everybody out of here right now," he replied.

"Wait a minute. Why do they have to leave?" Lorenz said, still drying his face.

The officer's voice climbed an octave, and he began to clap his large hands in rhythm with his words. "I don't have to answer your questions. I said everyone out. Now! This party is over!" The room began to grumble and a few kids complained under their collective breaths.

"This is bullshit. Y'all ain't got nothing better to do?" I shrieked.

The officer moved away from Lorenz and briskly glided over to me. "This party is disorderly, and it's disturbing the peace!" he screamed back.

I wondered what peace the officer was talking about since it was virtually nonexistent in that apartment complex. There wasn't peace when the boyfriend in apartment 3C placed a pillow over his girlfriend's face until she shook and died on an early Sunday morning before the old people headed out for church. There wasn't peace when my childhood friend, who lived in the building on the corner, was shot in the face while selling drugs outside of a city barber shop. There wasn't peace when Lorenz and I would get home after shooting hoops and see swarms of police cars blocking our doorway as they hunted for some black or brown culprit. *Peace, my ass*, I thought.

The spray from the officer's saliva sprinkled my nose when he spoke. It smelled of fresh coffee and cigars.

"Say one more word and I'm runnin' you downtown. You are startin' to get on my nerves," exclaimed the officer.

The room fell into an even deeper silence as my brain tussled with the options laid before me. I stood there wondering which audience I wanted to please, wobbling under the uncanny weight of cognitive dissonance, struggling to fight off the peer pressure, trying not to speak . . . *knowing* not to speak. The words came out anyway.

"This is bullshit," I repeated.

Suddenly, I felt the brunt of a heavy forearm slam into my chest. Panting for breath, I watched my arms flailing to secure myself. The once silent room erupted into a hodgepodge of shrieks and groans. Some of the kids leapt over the couch and tried to squeeze their bodies out of the first-floor window, knocking over dying houseplants and dollar store ashtrays. Sneakers and boots screeched on the floor. The officers wrestled a few of the potential escapees to the ground, forcing them to lay still. Feeling faint, I saw the girl who gave me the bag. Her slender body slipped out of the window and off into the darkness. It was then that I remembered what was in my back pocket. It was also then, at that very moment, that my life was altered by the presence of Afroprovidential redirection.

After the melee ended and the partygoers abandoned the premises, Lorenz and I were handcuffed and sitting on our knees in front of the building. The scratchy echo of radio dispatchers floated into the night air, and a quiet tear ran down my face. The officers, after talking in what resembled a football huddle, tossed their cigarettes on the ground and walked over to Lorenz and me.

"Get up," blurted the lead officer. The officer slowly unlocked the cuffs and pointed to the apartment door. Lorenz and I were afraid to move, afraid to think, afraid not to move or think.

"Go ahead," the cop repeated. "It's your lucky night. We got another call. No more time for this kiddie shit."

My feet were heavy in my boots, and my pants had fallen down to the point that they barely stayed around my waist. Lorenz and I walked to the apartment door and got inside. I took the bag of weed out of my pocket and flushed it down the toilet. Large, sticky clumps.

The night had ended. But it did not end with me being carted off to jail for holding drugs in my back pocket that were not mine. It did not end with me serving one to three years for possession of an illegal substance, or an endless collection of court dates, or watching my mother cry while I sat behind a plate of glass. The night did not end with a smudge on my record that would have ended my chances to receive federal scholarship funds for college. The night did not end with me tossed around the penal system like a sack of brown clay.

It did not end with me learning more about crime in prison than I knew outside its walls or working in the prison laundry for twenty cents a day. I was spared that night from myself, like so many other black and brown boys in a rush to make poor decisions. I experienced, firsthand, the taste of Afroprovidential redirection. There would be many more times when grace saved my life. There was an instance in a nightclub when I was twenty, and a boy about the same age pointed a gun directly at my forehead and promised to blow my head off. There was another incident when a high school friend and I were chased down a city street in D.C. by thugs with guns who thought we were someone else. There are too many times to remember. Yet the dust cleared, and by divine intervention, I am sitting in my office, staring at my diplomas, teaching Introduction to Business, writing this book, raising my children, loving my wife, breaking cycles, and moving onward, upward—a direct result of *Afroprovidential* redirection.

Chapter Thirteen

An Early Discernment
Racial Categorization

She gives me that puzzled look.
Her eyes aflame with wonder, arms folded across her chest.
"Daddy," she says.
I answer, "Yes, baby?"
"Am I black or white or both?"
I ease down in my chair and lower my glasses
so I can see the expression on her face.
"What do you mean, baby?" I ask again.
She says, "Mommy is white." She says, "You are black."
She tilts her head so her hair falls over her eye
"So, which one am I?"
"Well, which one do you think you are?"
She unfolds her arms and shifts her weight from the right leg to the left.
"I am both, and I am neither."
We smile together. She turns on her heels and leaves the room.
I smile because I love her . . .
Then I think
I am afraid for her life because she is black and white
and because I love her.

Chapter Fourteen

Transformation
A Discussion of Displaced Adulation

In my early teens, I remember being unconditionally consumed by basketball. Mother's nightly sacrament often consisted of dutifully prying a weather-beaten ball from the unyielding clutches of my brown, sleeping arms. Holding that ball, gripped between blackened fingertips and pressed tightly into my youthful chest, was like sleeping with a silent lover—a lover whose clandestine and slumbering kisses tasted of sweet, tawdry leather, sharing my bed on those sultry summer nights; she and I became one. Our hearts together drummed seventy-two beats per minute via a conjoined sinoatrial node, an amalgamated histology, drawing boy and game together.

In some respects, my intoxication with that ball was, at the very least, moderately constructive. Clearly, it was the presence of the game that shielded me from the evils that ran violently throughout the city streets. Not to recognize the inherently celestial distraction that basketball provided in my life would be an unconscionable oversight, a grave mistake. For it was through basketball I learned the merits of teamwork, synergy, creativity, and good old-fashioned ordered discipline, all of which should be central and imperative concepts to the life of a black boy. One needs to look no further, for example, than the lives of many black teens to recognize the apparent lack of emphasis on such ideals. Jails are saturated with young men of color who were never taught the absolute magnitude of social teamwork and/or personal discipline, and so they waste away, their bony legs sprawled across urine-stained mattresses, fighting to restrain sweat-stained tears ripping through their very souls as they huddle in a ball on a cold cement floor. They become a mere statistic—a number.

This is not to suggest that black youth are not victims of a host of social and economic maltreatments. Black and brown bodies, especially those who are inexperienced, male, and youthful, have been sociologically victimized since the birth of this nation. This is an effort to reiterate what occurs when they are not taught the most precious of lessons. While some black parents have equipped their children with an appropriate value system, others have not, and the proof is in the pudding. It is undeniable.

In returning, though, to my current and historical condition, it is quite easy to see that along with the aforementioned basketball-induced values and distractions followed a convoluted plethora of social fallout. Accordingly, it is only decades later I have come to distinguish basketball's true paradoxical influence on my overall development. Only now do I truly discern the truth and recognize the intricacies and dualities presented by the physical diversion I once held so dear. And after an extended succession of somewhat cathartic moments and therapeutic introspections, this reality has become scrupulously salient. A jolt of pristine clarity has led me to an unanticipated epiphany, and that epiphany has altered the very course of my life. I now see that my fidelity to the culture of basketball, to my silent lover, tremendously stunted my intellectual escalation. That's correct. Basketball has caused me cognitive harm. I find myself today, consequently, a miniaturized adaptation of what I should be. Although I now gallop with ferocious abandon, the truth remains that I will always be "catching up."

It is true my blessings are abundant. I am healthy, intact, and at least relatively well adjusted. But where could I have been had my earlier convictions not been dominated by the unremitting bouncing of a ball? How far could I have climbed, and how much time did I waste? How many narrow escapes did I nearly miss? I guess we will never know. In a trek to make up for lost time, in spite of what I will never discern, I now struggle to recover what I have missed out on. To the naked eye, it was simply a game. It was nothing more than a musical charade constructed by way of athletic pomp and circumstance. Yet with each dribble and shot, I now see that the game was actually played against me, not for me. I have not only been seductively deluded by a pastime but also hoodwinked by a fairly obscure yet societal normality. Basketball was the apparatus used, and I was the fool abused.

While the sport itself remains innocent, it is the manner basketball was forced on me that is the crime. To understand, we must look past the general physicality of basketball and allow our minds to peer at the game from a metaphorical and philosophical vantage point. We must uncover its cultural traps. We must allow ourselves the freedom to examine the sport's effects from a psychosocial standpoint. Only then can we admit to the following reality. Through the presence of the sport, I was systematically duped into what I call *displaced adulation*.

By my individual definition, displaced adulation is the commandingly destructive and ill-fated state that transpires when an individual or group of individuals is methodically cajoled into worshiping the acts of a specific person, group, thing, or entity. It is a construct mired in complexity, as it is challenging to identify and almost impossible to circumvent, for it leads to so many new questions. How does one evade the circumstances of his birth? How does one evade culture? How does a black boy repel his socially ordained destiny? The quandary germane to displaced adulation is not merely that society swindles one into following prescribed role models, for that hardly presents an insurmountable challenge and only scratches the surface.

In its most authentic form, the problem is that the preferred role models are not intellectually inspiring. Instead, they are simple, uneventful, undemanding, and regular. Let me be clear here. I do not propose *ordinary* is a dreadful word, nor do I recommend that *being regular* is a sin. Some of the world's most wonderful people define themselves as regular, and I clearly recognize the light and significance that regular folk bring to the world. To be an *everyday person*, as posited by Sly and the Family Stone, is a good thing.

There is an overwhelming sense of authenticity trapped within the souls of regular people. They ooze with a palpable validity. They are real, in the flesh, and in your face. I, however, argue that to strive for mediocrity and social regularity can often be a less than pleasing trait. Just because one is regular now does not suggest one should remain as such. Regularity should be transformative. In the end, it should be a stage, a brief stop along the winding route that is our lives. We should look back at our moments of regularity with passionate adoration, with nostalgia.

Whether we like it or not, most people are much too comfortable wearing their cloak of regularity. Mostly this happens because the models followed are, in fact, quite common in their own thinking and expectations. Frequently, those who we assign as role models fear stretching themselves, and the results are both distressing and noteworthy.

Displaced adulation adds to one's sociological propensity to secure role models that lack awe-inspiring intellectual proficiency, educational success, and cultural diversity. In many respects, the construct is the antithesis of Bandura's notion of self-efficacy in that it personifies low confidence. The laws of displaced adulation behoove one to revel in the mundane, dwell in the commonplace, and take refuge in the habitual—the consummate underachiever sulking in the shadows, afraid to abscond from life's labyrinthine tentacles, afraid to transgress normality, afraid to take a risk.

As the phrase dictates, one's adulation is customarily displaced, causing an individual to place love, trust, and faith in those who are devoid of hope. Displaced adulation is about falling in love with the superficial and altogether overlooking substance. It is about allowing oneself to be principally dislodged from one's own dreams and being told what is important instead of learning for one's self. It is about following the crowd, drowning in the mud of social hedonism, and succumbing to the soul-crushing weight of Orwellian Big Brother existence. Because of its subsistence, our world is full of zombie-like trolls dragging through life all the while afraid to move out of their own way. They choose to cut corners, hide in the shadows, and shy away from the things that might propel them into a new light.

Unlike many of the world's so-called social ills, displaced adulation tends to manifest incognito. Cryptic and venomous, it creeps like a masked monochrome vapor into the very crevices of one's soul, thus assassinating our collective probabilities to taste the sweetness of self-actualization.

Displaced adulation is a silent, nocturnal, nihilistic beast that strikes under the guise of a hushed reality, always primed for more blood. It is a meat eater. Its mere presence dethrones potential kings and queens before authentic growth can take form, prompting social death by way of mental asphyxiation. We see it seeping into our school systems and places of worship, and it rests its repulsive head on our very dinner tables. It is the reason our schools are dumbing down and our teachers are losing faith, yet it is so difficult for us to see. So hushed that its victim infrequently identifies its most repugnant effects, unaware of its esoteric covering.

More importantly, the dislodgement is both perpetuated and stimulated by those we love and shapes itself into silhouettes of friends, family, associates, and the like, very much in the form of emotional contagion. You have heard them. The mouths of its victims tend to utter phrases such as, "Why bother? Education won't change things," or, "Learning is a waste of time unless it pays you more money." I am sad to say phrases such as these are particularly ubiquitous in the black community.

In the spirit of practical application, let us reflect on my experience with displaced adulation as it sheds light on the power of this most dangerous ideal. My role models, the ones I chose to follow early on, were one-dimensional characters almost cardboard in nature. They pulsated in predictability and reveled in mediocrity. Their collective ideologies consisted of the narrowest perspectives. In short, they were untapped minds with potential, yet destined for nothing. This is not to say they were bad people, nor am I implying they did not possess positive traits. They were talented, humorous, quick-witted, and brazen.

My admiration for these individuals is just as authentic as it is for others because I clearly understand many of their challenges. I know who they are. I am simply stating that the skills I acquired by watching them, while developing with them, while breathing the same air circulating throughout the same neighborhood cocoon, were not helpful to my overall development. In fact, they were quite detrimental—even stifling. The reason the problem stings with reality is these individuals were seething with stunted energy, unable to unlock what held them back, unable to overcome the displacement, unable to energize their kinetic cathexis.

I was a self-proclaimed basketball junkie. For me, spending ten hours a day shooting hoops was hardly an extraordinary occurrence. Throughout my sandlot tenure, I gained quite a bit of respect from some of the older street-ballers, as they were affectionately called. For the most part, that motley crew consisted of numerous mythical figures of the blacktop who, for epigrammatic and particular moments, displayed astounding levels of athletic skill. They were colorful, compelling, loud, abrasive—beautifully dangerous. While waiting for my chance to play, I would eagerly watch from the sidelines, soaking in the midpoint of their every detail. With my youthful back pressed against the playground cage and the warm summer wind tickling my nose, I kept my eyes steady, watching them, loving them. I calculated their movements and imitated their pseudo-mannish bravado as they drank canned beer covered in crumpled paper bags in between afternoon games at the park. I would listen as their conversations permeated the air with soiled language, misogynist ideals, and sinful praises of money, taking it all in.

I grew more attracted with each passing moment. I floated on the rhythmic vibrations of their linguistic appeal, as my prime desire was to be like them. I wanted to look like them. I wanted to saunter about, almost carelessly, as if the world was nothing more than a colossal playground constructed for the manifestation of cultural machismo. I wanted to speak before I thought and toss vulgarities with noteworthy precision. I wanted to spit on the street, grab my crotch, and wink at the honey-brown teenage flowers blooming outside the court's edges. I wanted to bask in the anti-utilitarian calculus of the street.

What is even more interesting is that my psychological makeup remained in stark contrast to that which I wanted to become. I longed to be beautifully dangerous. For in truth, I was nothing like my peers. Pretending to be hard, I dragged my soft and puerile sensitivities like concealed luggage hidden deep in the inner sanctum of my chocolate soul, pretending, contorting my mental limbs so they might fit within a neat and tidy box—a social box created to entrap. Inside, my emotions were packed tightly together, crammed inside my consciousness and always outwardly repelling my inclination to smile, to do anything that represented weakness, to be tougher than my chi demanded, to lie.

Little did I know the transformation had already begun. My choice had been made, but why those models? Why didn't I choose my teachers, dentist, pastor, or father to worship? What about the many others surrounding me? I am sure I missed several positive sorts waiting in the wings. Why wasn't I drawn to the intellectual members of my community? Why weren't they considered cool? Why didn't I follow the path of the women in my life? Was this regarded as unacceptable, and did it go against the unwritten machismo code? Could my community, my nation, or my world predetermine who I would become? Had a plan been previously set? In retrospect, my answer is a definitive *yes*.

The problem is that I was socially notified, without my permission by the way, as to what I could and would become. This apparent notification, whisking through the air of my community like a wordless whisper, modified my destiny and determined my fate. When I looked around, where did I see those who looked like me? I saw reflections of myself in the courtroom, but seldom rearing the gavel. I saw images of me in school, but rarely teaching the class. I saw visions of me in the boardroom, but always cleaning up the office with a mop and bucket.

It was only on the playground where I saw depictions of the attainable. There, I saw a basketball player: beautiful, brown, kinetic, but unwittingly limited. Dancing in a sightless stupor, I meandered down the same yellow brick road as many did before me, always listening first and reacting later. I was lost in reverie.

I took notice as society told me that my key to eminence and affluence was the uncanny knack to put a little orange ball into a rusted basket, so I practiced doing so until the soles of my high-tops splintered into numerous pieces of fractured rubber and broken string. I played until my calloused toes burned at the tips. I listened as society told me that muscularity was analogous to masculinity, so I lifted weights until my body was a chiseled figure of hardened onyx: stalwart in shape, yet feeble in mind.

Society also told me the clothing I wore while playing ball on the playground could lift me to novel altitudes. I spent every penny I earned from summer jobs on overpriced, name-brand apparel, all in a quest for cultural commonality. Trading in the lineage of my last name for a brand, I hunted for the latest thing, pimped by propaganda. Like so many in my clique, I was a branded animal falling into the pits of psychological and subliminal consumerism. I sought the elusive Joneses, all the while allowing my so-called internal happiness to be dominated by my collection of tangible possessions, none of which I could truly afford.

I looked the part, yet I missed the point. Reading was for nerds; writing was out of the question. The inability to visualize the disheartening cheerless milieu of my dilemma aided my sickened state. I was doing what I was told, listening to the omnipotent forces that be, heeding that muted insinuation.

Of course, there were also forces pulling in the other direction in attempts to get me to see the light, fighting against the current of displaced adulation. Although many were black, they were exceedingly outnumbered. My father, a brilliant artist in his own right, filled my head with anecdotes of the political upheavals of the 1960s. On several occasions, he forced me to sit and listen to the revolution-ridden melodies of Bob Dylan, Gil Scott-Herron, and Richie Havens. Elongating my horizons, pushing his antiquated eyeglasses above his nose, he would look over my head when he spoke, listening to a soundtrack I could not hear as if watching his memories on a screen I could not see.

My father's jeans were covered with paint in his art-studio basement; the smoldering waft of incense filled the house and set the scene. Smiling, he would rub his hairy face and reach into a dusty milk crate, slowly lifting another album over his head. "Oh, yeah," he would mutter. "You gotta hear this one, son." He would place the needle on the record, smile, and rest his back against the wood paneling, trying to conceal the remnants of marijuana slipping through his hippie veins. His feet would dangle over the chair, exposing the brownness of his socks. We would sometimes listen to Woody Guthrie's folk tales of fascism, foodless days, and limited opportunities. Other days, we would listen to Marvin Gaye or Curtis Mayfield swoon about black love and sexual healing. Bill Withers and Paul Simon. Joe Cocker and James Brown. On some nights, we would talk for hours, reliving his exciting days of afros, bell-bottoms, Hồ Chí Minh, and the struggle to be seen as a man. He would tell me of his military days in Cuba, Joan Baez, and The Last Poets. We argued about political science, social science, and environmental science. Fleetwood Mac and Bob Marley. We wrestled with racism, sexism, and racist sexism. Muddy Waters and Aretha Franklin. We talked, and it was beautiful.

Today, I recognize my father's efforts to plant a seed of hopeful harvest. At the time, those were just words trickling from the bearded mouth of an interesting, albeit anachronistic, man, and so my revelations were fleeting. His ideas were of an antediluvian tongue—almost prehistoric to my infantile and unapprised ears. Unlike him, I subsisted on the watery current of unassuming youth, and the days of old had little effect. My essence hankered chiefly for that little orange ball and the characters who came with it, and what a cast of characters they were.

I can still see their faces wavering through the watery dreamscape mist in my mind's eye. There was Black Rich, ceaselessly smiling through his snow-white teeth. His skin seemed to glimmer in the summer sun like scorched tar dipped in malted licorice. Rich's body was elongated and nimble. Regardless of his astute knack for hurling infective comedic-style narratives about all of our mothers, his failure to take advantage of his athletic preeminence was legendary. High school coaches drooled when Rich swayed through the halls, eager to add his illustrious skill set to their collective rosters. Their eyes would appraise his streamlined body, quietly examining as if Rich were standing on some dust-ridden slave block dripping in the watery clank of iron shackles. If they could, they would have grabbed the underside of his blackened chin and tussle his face close to theirs so they might inspect his teeth. They would run their hands down the darkened curvature of his back, buttocks, and muscular calves, all the while imagining yet another horse in their stable, another tool moving them ever closer to a coaching position at the college level.

Walking to a class he normally avoided, Rich's rail-thin arms drooped nonchalantly around one of his teenage female admirers, soaking in the still puddle of the moment. He seemed to revel in being himself, sucking up the youthful yet fleeting admiration of all that comes with adolescent popularity, the momentary in-crowd as well as all that comes with naïve exuberance, charismatic attractiveness, and unbelievable athletic talent. Yet his true dream—to be a member of the team—was thwarted by his failure to identify the correlation between education and sports, a clear symptom of displaced adulation.

Rich was a pretender. He pretended to be confident. He pretended to be intact. He pretended he did not spend his nights with his face mashed into a tearstained pillow, longing to play for a team for which he could not qualify. The muddled sobs seeping through the crack under his door would drift into his mother's corner room and awaken her from her slumber. Hearing his sobs, but exhausted from a fifteen-hour workday waiting tables, she would turn on her side, sigh, and drift back to sleep, trying to forget the pain locked inside her son's chest. The pain of pretending.

Rich proceeded to pretend but could not escape the truth. To perform his hoops artistry on the high school squad, Rich would need a 2.0 grade point average and a relatively acceptable attendance rate. As it happened, he accomplished neither of these tasks. To conceal his disappointment, he would cast transparent aspersions toward the coach and reiterate his lack of interest in the entire process. In the end, it didn't matter that he ran like a gazelle when he had the ball in his hand. It made no difference that he could hurdle would-be defenders via the springs attached to his feet. Unwilling to chart a new course, a course supported by the powers of didactic progress, Rich dropped out of high school. He had several babies by several different women, jumped from one job to the next, but he still tells the most amusing mother jokes one could ever imagine. A magnificent soul, a pristine black spirit, compressed by the burden of displaced adulation and trapped in a prism of self-induced intellectual mediocrity. Yet he is only one of the many names among names.

Now, at age thirty-nine, I see society's prescribed expectations for me were not expectations. They were, to my newfound chagrin, limitations. I was being led, as was Black Rich, like the proverbial horse in pursuit of the carrot that dangles in front of its head. To my vexation, I now recognize that the carrot was nothing more than a metaphorical and figurative tease, driving my unremitting descent toward adult idleness. With my eyes steadfast on the dangling passion fruit, I could not see the makings of the peripheral world. When I finally did notice a glimpse of what was out there, the forces of displaced adulation pulled me back in, hog-tied by my ankles, and returned me to a place in which I dwelled.

Athletics were my designated ticket to a self-perpetuated and tangential nirvana. I didn't realize I was just doing what was expected of me, always feeding into the cyclical fiasco that turns at a breakneck pace throughout my community. I was an anti-trailblazer. Why did I not see the brown, white, yellow, and female intellectuals? I am sure they were there. Why did I miss them despite the fact they were screaming my name through books, graves, journals, and the heavens above?

Again, following the codifications of my current cultural condition, I missed the point. As far as I was concerned, black boys did not read, write, or think. They played basketball. Black boys did not dream of becoming literary legends. They practiced to become playground legends. Although I was never told these truths directly, I listened to the undeclared whispers of American culture until the cumulative effect took its toll. All intellectual fires that burned within me had been covered with a dampened blanket.

This essay, in the spirit of introspective inquiry, is an attempt to contest the ever-growing threat of displaced adulation, not to mention it is proof that the effects of this harmful social illness can be reversed. You see, my friend, there is a cure. This is my effort to break through those miserable obstructions and wretched blockades set to impede my cognitive progress as well as the progress of those to come.

The thoughts of this essay smolder like scorched wood as they percolate steam into my mind's eye; they remind me of lost time and missed opportunities. They remind me of the current state of myriad precious minds yet to be set free. They remind me of the fiery dilemmas germane to tradition, custom, and cultural digressions. I now see the pipedream in which I unknowingly lived. Sports should not be the only metaphorical rope that heaves black men out of the perilous concrete jungle, and yet many times it is. Whose fault is this? Who is to blame?

The desire and pursuit for knowledge is the preeminent way to break through societal barricades, and it is the most authentic medicine for social and spiritual illness. It is up to us to erect a change powered by intellectual mobility. All progress begins in the mind. Although we can never know everything, it is an ethical misfortune to limit ourselves to our immediate surroundings.

I hope that my words cross all racial, partisan, and cultural lines. Despite our respective and selective communities or races, we all often look to the wrong people for philosophical guidance. I would also add, though, that it does the African American even more harm since the cards are already negatively stacked. As noted on several occasions by Dr. Cornel West, we are all cracked vessels. Black people do not have a moratorium or monopoly on displaced adulation. We all, at one time or another, fail to see our true potentials. My firm belief is if we, in a communal sense, challenge ourselves, grapple for knowledge, and learn from our most gifted thinkers, we will be much better off for the effort. Study, thought, meticulous introspection, and personal inquiry are what the greatest of thinkers do. For the sake of humankind, we need to do the same.

We must respect the minds and actions of those who dare to think in an age when thought is overwhelmed by groupthink, group-shift, and group-thoughtlessness. I am afraid the present era has failed to prepare properly our youngest minds for cognitive acceleration. Today, we have a world permeated with robotic and drone-like underachievers. We have to end this perpetual state of non-academic madness.

While the concepts of street smarts and common sense have their respective places within the overall discourse, it is foolhardy to pretend education, traditional or otherwise, is unnecessary or outdated. More important, it is dangerous to believe one can be overeducated. *What a ridiculous notion.* The synthesis of these ideals makes one whole, and the most valuable means of ensuring the continued existence of humanity is profoundly dependent upon how we manipulate our educational talents. We cannot be duped into a society that emphasizes blind followership. Individual intellect and leadership should be our keys to progress. Our leaders must be controversial, passionate, and most importantly possess the power of high-level thought. To place emphasis on the mind should not be looked at as a feat of elitism. When did it become negative to be intelligent?

Still young, relatively speaking, I feel that time has yet to eradicate my chance to amend my once-prescribed route. It is not too late to remove the blinders and see all that is around me. I now read with an insatiable hunger, cleaving through the mutton of unknown subjects like a ravenous carnivore, feasting on the written word, slaving to its essence. Delving into matters far removed from basketball, I have developed an addictive and unquenchable passion to learn. I have been scholastically set ablaze, and the fire burns incessantly. Regardless of the newfound rigor in which I study all things possible, I have never been so self-actualized. I cannot imagine going back to the way I used to be—to that barren place where body dictates mind and each day is wasted on being average, back to the constant bouncing of a rubber ball and the blankness of an unchallenged mind, back to those sultry nights holding that silent, weather-beaten lover in my arms. This is not to infer that playing basketball is vile; it is to solidify that *only* playing basketball is vile. There is so much more to life. There is so much more to learn, and this perspective must be provided to those standing at the precipice.

Today, I sincerely comprehend what Plato meant when he wrote, "If a man genuinely wishes to learn, he sees in the course marked out for him a path of enchantment which he must strain every nerve to follow or die in the attempt. When this conviction has taken possession of him, he never ceases to practice such habits as will make him an intelligent student able to reason soberly by himself."

In the spirit of Plato, I have become infatuated with self-improvement through scholarly means. I recognize the key to my lifelong happiness is interrelated with the ability to grow as a student of life. There is power in the elixir of both traditional and non-traditional learning. Mixed into my ferocity for interdisciplinary reading, I have completed several master's degrees, and I am currently working toward a second doctorate. I do not proclaim this as a means to show off or place myself on a pedestal. Again, the objective is to buttress the certainty that displaced adulation is hardly a death sentence. It can be corrected, as it has been in my life. Once it is corrected, true potential becomes limitless.

I have recently set a goal to obtain several more doctorates, to read several hundred books, to teach several hundred college classes, and to change several hundred lives. Notwithstanding the streetballers who would most likely define these goals as wasteful and absurd, I now realize the power and outright audacity of such an objective. I now see the power truly resides within the walls of my inner being. If I wish to expand, it is up to me. Triumph is but a few books and creative thoughts away.

Despite what society often promotes, the idea is not to learn as a means for accumulating monetary wealth or fiscal advantage. I recognize a PhD does not ensure a comfortable income and the obtainment of a home loan will not necessarily hinge on an acquired piece of paper. My point is that higher education should not be a monetary investment. Knowledge via education is a privilege and a calling. I imagine, given the state of the world economy, there are countless brilliant and educated people earning minimum wage and struggling under the unbearable weight of student loans, housing bills, and the like.

Education is much larger in breadth than vocational tenure. It is about replacing ignorance with knowledge. It is about becoming an engaged participant of life-related history rather than merely surveying from the sidelines. Education allows one to hold intimate conversations about astronomy with Galileo and theological debates with Descartes. It allows one to squabble with Du Bois and rumble with Mahatma—all in real time, of course. It displays the horror of man's misdeeds and the gaiety of his brilliance. To be educated is to unleash one's potential for becoming more than *ordinary*.

While some downplay education, its true power cannot be denied, and there is truth in the Duboisian notion of the talented tenth. Not just a brown talented tenth, but one as colorful as the world's combined diaspora. Educational systems, when operated fairly, control the future of the world, dictate the solvency of our national security, and set the stage for the evolving global community. It is true, however, that problems surface when the very system that was created to promote self-improvement becomes so riddled with corruption it causes distress and harm to the masses.

American education has its positive traits, and I do not mean to state otherwise. It must be noted, however, that countless bureaucratic, racist, and sexist influences often taint even the most wonderful of creations. Accordingly, education must remain pure and ethical. In light of my various musings, I stress the following point: knowledge is much lovelier than money. It smells of uncultivated roses and tickles the very taste buds of my mind. Even more important, it is deeply intertwined with my personal dreams. I seek, you see, a *wealth of the mind*. I seek a condition by which novel abstractions become a mainstay and where I can exist on the sheer prevalence of what can be learned. In other words, I wish to fill each crevice of my brain with high-quality information. I wish to brawl with the thorniest and most obstinate ideas, ranging from science to classical literature. From Kant to Marx, I want to know it all.

For me, knowledge is the wonder of the chase that makes life worth living. While some race for dollars and medals, I have chosen to race for intellect and wisdom. My wealth pushes me to understand the incomprehensible and to answer questions yet to be asked. Just as Albert Einstein noted throughout his life, the idea is to think as God would think, to move past one's mortal and flimsy flesh, and to use the mind as it was intended. The brain, the most intricate and underutilized mechanism, needs to be pushed, shaped, and pushed again. Accordingly, my dreams rest in the wane of books, ideas, words, and knowledge.

My goals, however, do not stop there. Why should they? Why should I not strive to reach every educational peak available? Surpassing displaced adulation opens one's eyes to greater heights. After I complete my formal education, I wish to become a constant learner, teacher, writer, and defender of the pursuit of wisdom. Throughout this most surprising progression of Frankenstein proportions, I realize what I am becoming.

It feels good to let the cat out of the bag. I can discard those old, burdensome weights of black scholastic ineptitude that haunted me during elementary school and followed me to college. I can shed the humiliation of knowing I only went to college strictly to play a sport, and I flunked out several times due to a lack of effort and sheer laziness. I can be released from the embarrassment that once came with wanting to be smart and black at the same time, now understanding the concepts are not mutually exclusive. I can smile in the light of something good; I can be happy to learn.

When I'm quiet and the ears of my soul are alert, I can hear my mind shifting like tectonic plates, moving ever so silently in search of an intellectual connection. The change is monumental, and I can feel its rumblings. I bask in this most soulful of alterations, for I, with pride, am becoming a black intellectual. Somewhat Darwinian in form, I am evolving into a higher species. With this evolution, new role models multiply with every book I read. In one way or another, each displays a host of social, cultural, and philosophical differences. Nonetheless, through the rigors of reflective insight, they have aroused a combustible inferno within me. They have proven, without a doubt, the search for wisdom is the most moving force outside of God that exists. They have not only transcended their respective fields, they have also replaced my old and quite ordinary role models. My new models are Russian, Celtic, and female. Others are as black as I am and have forever changed the image of the academic landscape. They all unfasten fresh vicinities within my mind and encourage me to attain more than basketball ever did.

Who are these enchanted souls who dwell among print, periods, and quotation marks? They are my new best friends. They are Aristotle, Heidegger, Baldwin, Nabokov, Adler, Machiavelli, Dickinson, Marx, Weber, and Dyson. They are Angelou, Hurston, Tolstoy, Gaskins, Cose, Piaget, and Taylor. They are Cleaver, Morrison, Chomsky, and Friedman. They are nothing alike, yet they are exactly alike. Thanks to each of these individuals as well as those like them, the bar has been raised. Jumping ten feet through the air and dunking a ball at one time seemed so deity-like to my youthful eyes. In comparison to those I have studied as of late, the former seems like a mere carnival trick.

I still see the beauty in the slam dunk, but it no longer compares to the radiant brilliance of those who stretch the boundaries of thought. There is a brightened and shimmering reflection surrounding the ideas of my new role models, and I am amazed at the rapid growth of my new family. It seems each book consummates yet another birth, thus increasing the size of my adopted clique. My generational lineage is in motion, and I dare not cease its movement. Learning is truly generational.

I have fallen in love with the words of the proverbial thinker, notwithstanding the perspectives he or she may defend. It is not about what is said but how literary ideals are defended. For me, the potential of the written word is more powerful than any athletic achievement, for nothing is more transcendent than the concept of thought. It is the ability to improve my thoughts I hold so dear.

The greatest thoughts are to be used to create even greater thoughts. This is why we must change the paradigm regarding whom we follow. We must learn from and listen to those who covet the audacity of new ideas. That being said, the subsequent sections of this book delve into the deepest corners of my mind, unleashing the thoughts of a man swirling in a controlled, educational dervish. The topics, no matter how varied, will always support the following realization: humankind has a duty to study the teachings of those who have come before, and it is my pledge to do just that. Neither I nor the world in which I live have any more time for games. My passions are linked to the ideas that originated before my existence, thus laying the groundwork, cementing the social foundations on which we exist. Our problems have compounded exponentially, and education may very well be the solution to our societal demise.

Chapter Fifteen

Black the Way I Want to Be

Like a piece of human elastic,
I often leave this monotonous pace and arrive into my abstract place
Where time is still
And no blood spills
Where hills are flat and the sun shares the sky with men who fly
And I like it there
That place where I can be black the way I want to be
No binding racial limitations
And with the power of my thought
I create landslides of onslaughts
Taking brain vacations
Despite the history of hatred in this nation
And yet it seems reality can't compete with dreams
So I stay constantly fixed on blue
That blue uniform—the one the killer wears
The killer with the badge and pistol
That killer who brings me back to the place where I am a mere brown lump
Of inhumanity
And where my reality says I will die by his hands

Chapter Sixteen

The Learning of Racial Mythologies and the DNA Conundrum

Are You Sure You're White?

What is race? Why is race so important in America? How does the idea of race shape our individual and collective mindsets? What factors determine what our race is? Several months ago, during a class at the University of Maryland, I presented my students with each of these questions. The responses were both compelling and controversial—so compelling, in fact, that the conversation continued thirty minutes after the class session ended. It spilled out into the crowded campus hallways, seeped into the student lounge, and eventually found its way into the campus cafeteria and faculty breakroom.

As I listened to the students barter racial ideologies like sheep or oxen, it became quite evident to me that race is a construct mired in social untruths. More importantly, the longer the students challenged one another, the more obvious it became they knew very little about what constitutes an individual's race. Now, it is important to state here that the students in my classes are highly intelligent, hardworking, and goal-oriented individuals. They are a joy to teach, and I would be lying if I told you they did not expand my intellectual horizons on a daily basis. The students' lack of racial knowledge was, in actuality, what I liken to racial miseducation, *indoctrination personified*. We will delve into this point later. For now, however, let me just say most Americans tend to conceptualize their racial makeup in ways that are overtly elementary, extremely oversimplified, and emotionally driven. For them, race is a visceral construct. It feeds like a ravenous beast on feelings and behaviors, always pulling and tugging at our instinctual nature. Our behavioral reactions associated with race tend to cause knee-jerk responses based primarily on a myriad of stereotypes. If my class, from an attitudinal standpoint, could be considered a microcosm of this nation, which I do believe it is, then the proof is in the pudding; Americans have no real idea what race actually is, where race actually comes from, or what differentiates one race from another.

Now, it would be one thing if most Americans were open to discussing their various misconceptions or delusions regarding race. This rarely happens because most of us actually think we know all there is to know about race, especially our own. We assume we are experts, shored up by the notion that our individual racial experiences are all we need to solidify our expertise on the matter. This is why so many black folks tend to think they know everything about blackness. This is also why so many white Americans think they know everything about whiteness. In truth, though, how can every black man or woman claim to know what another black person feels, thinks, or envisions about their race? How can a single white man or woman do the same? More importantly, how can each group mandate racial standards regarding good versus bad race behavior (within their own group)? Don't get me wrong. I clearly understand the reasons why black solidarity exists. There is something to be said for coming together in times of crisis and supporting the rights of black people. But while it is obvious, for instance, that black people share a plethora of sociological and historical experiences, how can we assume each and every black person responds to those experiences in exactly the same way? Additionally, how can we determine what those responses should be? Where does blackness or whiteness start and individuality begin? A very tough set of questions indeed, but ones that need to be pondered.

In getting back to the previous point, black and white Americans tend to act as if they have acquired a supernatural propensity to determine the sociobehavioral underpinnings of their own racial cohorts. Americans almost never stop to reconcile the absurdity of conducting racial psychotherapy on themselves. They rarely scrutinize, for instance, their introspective methodologies or the various problems associated with racial self-diagnosis. For in truth, the inner self is almost always confused by the outer self. To understand race, from a holistic perspective, we must get outside ourselves and seek to find the truth as it relates to how the concept of race became important to human beings in the first place. This begins by grappling with the definition of race while also examining the concept from its proper historical context.

The various mystifications relevant to our individual realizations of race are only part of the problem. Unlike the former issue, which suggests we are often psychologically reluctant or sociologically incapable of thinking honestly and effectively about our own so-called race, it is also true that most of our racial perceptions are overwhelmingly attached to an aesthetic. We tend to dwell on the surface when thinking about race. In other words, we let our eyes tell us what race is. This is problematic because eyes, in and of themselves, are not equipped to decipher the convoluted labyrinth of American racial reality. The eyes are tricksters. They play games. They are merely a set of biological human utensils, and although they play a very critical part in the goings and comings of our daily lives, eyes do not think or contemplate. The eyes are unable to calculate that there is no single or particular trait that distinguishes or separates one so-called race from another. In fact, if you were to select two human beings at random and place their DNA into a Petri dish, you would quickly discover both individuals share over 99 percent of the same DNA. Moreover, if you were to select the DNA of a caveman and compare it to that of a modern man, both subjects would also share over 99 percent of the same DNA. Since science has agreed DNA represents the foundational building blocks of biological humanity, it becomes quite clear we are much more the same, biologically speaking, than we are different. In fact, our sameness is overwhelming. DNA research suggests human beings are a racially evolving anthology of rainbow twins and quintuplets, inhaling and exhaling by the millions. Roaming in massive herds of humanity, we are chiefly tied together by strings of organic fabric. If anything, race is merely a synthetic sociological construct fashioned within the imperfect minds of human beings who have already lived, already learned, and already died. It is perpetuated by man's desire to see himself in line with his peers, to demarcate levels of human existence.

Whether or not we realize it, our racial identity is inextricably connected to what we have learned about ourselves. Learning is the key. It is the breeding ground. It is the alpha and omega of all racial self-identification. We shall discuss the relationship between race and learning later. For now, however, it is important to recognize that what the world says about one's racial makeup is often scientifically incorrect. I realize for many of us the aforementioned points might seem a bit far-fetched. We might find ourselves pushing back against the contextual validity and theoretical reliability of such unconventional positions. Don't fret, dear reader, as your disbelief is quite understandable. Recalibrating racial codifications can be a counterintuitive exercise. The uneasiness that fills the spirit at this stage must be leveraged with truth. Truth that highlights the reality that race is not a biological fact, *it is a learned phenomenon*, cultivated and solidified over time. Race is an infinite precept that expands as individuals expand, always in conjunction with social and generational development. Race, dear reader, is an idea.

For most of us, race is something that begins at one point and ends at another. We think of race as if it were a sprint or a contest that originates at a definitive starting point and stops at a prescribed destination. Such thinking, though, is incongruous because race is not a linear construct. It does not travel in a straight line. Nor is there a clear-cut, unambiguous, or stationary way of thinking about race. Instead of progressing in a straight line, race vibrates and twitches like a seizing heart. Always in motion, it thrusts and inflates with a continuous fluidity. Due to mankind's nomadic sexual predilections, it is a scientific impossibility for any given person to be considered a single so-called race. The combinations of human beings who have procreated since the beginning of time is quite expansive, and whether we like it or not, blacks have consistently mated with whites, whites have consistently mated with browns, and browns have consistently mated with yellows.

Also, the idea of race is relatively new. Up until the fourteenth century, people tended to establish demarcations based primarily on language, wealth, gender, religion, and geography. It was much more important, so to speak, if a person were a man or woman. The word race, as we know it, was not even introduced into the English language until the fifteenth or sixteenth century, thus launching its modern socio-political significance and altering the very way we interact with one another. While it is true racial attacks and cultural mistreatment did occur in the early centuries, the majority of such occurrences were associated more with tribalism. Racism existed, to be sure, but its presence was much different from what it is today. Historically speaking, human beings obviously recognized skin and eye color or hair texture and face shape, but the idea of classifying these physical differences into obstinate taxonomies did not come until later—much later. We will deal more with that fact in a bit. For now, though, we must remember physical distinctions can be misleading because they do not necessarily fall along prescribed racial lines. Consequently, to hypothesize one's race based on skin color or hair texture or eye shape is an impractical thing to do. We have to remember human beings are ceaselessly moving about, bubbling and percolating, establishing a wide diaspora of multiethnic offspring. As a result of this pervasive state of wanderlust, today there are so-called black people with straight hair, hazel eyes, and thin noses who were born in the deepest sections of Mexico. There are so-called white people, on the other hand, with coarse, curly hair, dark brown eyes, and wide noses who were born in the Middle East. What about the biracial and/or multiracial couples who marry and cross-pollinate with other biracial individuals? Do we classify an African-American woman with a Chinese father as Asian, or do we need to know much more about her parents, grandparents, and great grandparents to answer such a riddle? What about a fair-skinned South African woman born in Johannesburg to a Jamaican mother and Iranian father? What about the so-called white Russian man who has children with the Afro-German woman born on European soil. Is this enough data to determine race and which takes precedence, whether it is land or origin or so-called racial cohort? How far back do we have to go to determine when the original so-called race stream begins in a given bloodline? Are there even enough racial categories for all of us to fit into, and more importantly, who has the power to establish these categories? Who sets the course? To further complicate the matter, there are individuals who are considered white when visiting one hemisphere and brown when in another hemisphere. That same individual, however, can travel to yet another country and be deemed as black. When a so-called white woman is impregnated by a so-called black man and gives birth to twins who are different colors, what race are the babies? Can twins born at the same time belong to two different races? What does the world say about these kids when they walk down the street together, and does the perception of the world supersede one's DNA? What about those so-called black individuals who are fair enough in complexion to pass for white (as wonderfully highlighted in Philip Roth's *The Human Stain*)? Are these classifications fair? Are they real? How many people lie about their races to their children, further complicating self-identities, and how do we keep track of such instances? Who is responsible for cultivating these codifications, and at what point do we run out of possible racial segmentations?

Although mankind has tried to divide the aforementioned examples into strict racial categories, the segmentations have been based upon false standards, poor science, unclear rules, fake histories, and uninformed traditions. All of these are learned over time, which brings us back to one of my earlier points. To understand racial divisions, we need to begin with the concept of learning. Why do I say this? I say this because *race is learned*. Race is something that is understood and recognized over time, which eventually leads to a relatively permanent change in our behavior. By seeing things anew, learning becomes a process of gaining perspective through experience. Why is this important? Well, as we acknowledge this definition, we can begin to appreciate that human beings learn race in some of the same ways they learn other ideals in life. Just as one learns, for instance, that touching a hot stove leads to a burnt finger or that one plus one equals two, one also learns being dark skinned with coarse hair and full lips means one is black, and being black, in turn, can lead to a host of socio-economical and behavioral circumstances. The progression, then, is somewhat systematic. As the learning process unfurls, we are introduced to a phenomenon, we get comfortable with the phenomenon, we see the phenomenon in action, we adopt the parameters of the phenomenon, we apply the phenomenon, and then we allow that phenomenon to shape our thoughts and actions.

LEARNING THEORY 101

If we were to scan academic literature, we would surely uncover a vast assortment of models and theories linked to learning and behavior. One that seems to fit rather seamlessly with our current discussion of race is typically referred to as social learning theory. Created by Canadian-American social scientist Albert Bandura, former head of the American Psychological Society, this theory posits people learn by watching, copying, and reacting to peers, friends, and folks they find intellectually or emotionally appealing. Bandura suggests the learner molds themselves in such a way that they not only identify with a particular peer group but, in some cases, wish they and the peer were one and the same. Under the rubric of social learning theory, learning is primarily observational. It is safe to assume racial identity can be learned in the same way. When we are young, we observe the various racial labels ascribed to us. We become attracted to or comfortable with individuals who heavily personify and promote the said label. We then apply this label in an everyday setting, and we eventually and overwhelmingly conform to the rules and regulations germane to that label.

It is important to point out that the individuals who teach us right from wrong may or may not be right or wrong themselves. The ethical calculus germane to race is hardly a zero-sum game. This is critical because it highlights the fact that many of us may learn how to be white (whatever that may entail) from people who have no idea what being white is. For some white people, the goals of whiteness include listening to certain types of music, attending certain types of events, eating certain types of foods, and adhering to a particular set of social standards. Social learning theory suggests that to learn whiteness from an individual who believes the aforementioned ideals enhances the chances the learner will accept these ideals. Ultimately, we become a given race because we follow those who teach us what it means to be a member of that race.

Whereas social learning theory seems to dovetail nicely with our example of how people learn race, there are other learning theories that work equally as well. Each theory, incidentally, further supports the aforesaid interaction between learning, behavior, and racial identification. That said, let's turn our attention to classical conditioning. In the 1890s, famed physiologist Ivan Pavlov conducted a series of experiments on dogs. By and large, Pavlov recognized that dogs learned by creating and establishing cognitive relationships between stimuli. When Pavlov introduced meat powder to dogs, for instance, he noticed the dogs would salivate when they saw the meat powder. Over time, though, the dogs became conditioned in such a way they no longer needed to see the meat powder to salivate. Soon, the dogs salivated (in preparation for food) when they attached (mentally) various other symbols to being fed. Consequently, this process is referred to today as *classical conditioning*. It is obvious how the classical model of learning can be applied to the way we learn race. Not only are we conditioned, over time, to learn what race consists of, but we later develop cognitive connections between what race represents to us, how our so-called racial cohort is *supposed* to act, and why we fall into that particular racial category in the first place. In some cases, the symbols (or connections between stimuli) lead to our ability to further integrate ourselves into the cultural nuance of a given racial group. This line of thinking might account for those black or white people who follow racial paradigms simply because they feel as if they had no other choice.

Altogether, the Pavlovian approach to learning is highly regarded in academic, professional, managerial, and psychological communities. For that matter, so is social learning theory. Nonetheless, each of these models is far from perfect. One of the arguments against the classical ideal, for instance, is it focuses primarily on involuntary learning. In other words, Pavlov's experiments hinged on when and what caused the dogs to salivate. Salivation, though, is an involuntary physical reaction. We salivate in biological preparation to eat. We can't control this salivation; it just happens. Since classical conditioning does not necessarily address learning that occurs on purpose and with intent, there are some who argue against the broader validity of the model. This is important to understand in relation to the way human beings often learn race because there are those of us who do learn race on purpose. We actively reach out, trying to understand where we belong and who we are. Our efforts are voluntary. They are done on purpose. This nuance, however, is addressed by B.F. Skinner's learning model of *operant conditioning,* which takes the overall learning process a few steps further, beyond involuntary learning and to a place where and when we learn with intent. But who is Skinner and how does his learning model relate to race?

B.F. Skinner, throughout his esteemed psychological career (ranging roughly from the 1940s to the 1980s), used various techniques and approaches to support the premise that learning does not only come about by way of conditioning. He claimed learning must be considered in terms of its affiliation to rewards and punishments. The general idea of his approach, which can also apply at least indirectly with hedonistic theory, suggests people learn by reacting to things they desire and things they do not desire. Skinner concluded that an individual's specific motivations become more prominent as they learn over time, but they are overwhelmingly affected by positive and negative reinforcement. He employed quite a few experimental methodologies to test his ideas and was ultimately confident in his findings. In conjunction with the previous learning models, we can easily see the correlation between operant conditioning and the manner in which we learn race. The Skinnerian approach claims when we actively seek to know what so-called race we belong to, we begin to distinguish the consequences and rewards pertinent to finding the answer. In other words, it becomes painstakingly clear to us that knowing one's racial identity is a very important step in our personal and social development. Furthermore, when we can appropriately exemplify we have accepted our race, we are rewarded with the self-satisfaction of reaching a major milestone and being admitted to a racial cohort. Social acceptance is a powerful learning tool. Self-identification becomes analogous with pleasure and reward. Conversely, though, we also recognize early on not knowing our race (or disagreeing with our racial grouping) leads to mockery, ridicule, subjugation, and the like. This subjection process is what I refer to as *ethno-excommunication* (the act of being ousted from a given racial/ethnic demographic due to differences in perspective or the inability to determine what race one supposedly belongs to). Sadly, ethno-excommunication tends to increase the chances the individual will suffer emotionally, socially, and psychologically.

In keeping with the Bandurian, Pavlovian, and Skinnerian schools of thought, one could go even farther and suggest we also copy what we have learned about our so-called race, only to further propagate these ideas as we get older and teach those who come after us. The propagation process includes, naturally, our decision to fit in and adopt tendencies associated with a specific racial cohort. You see, when it comes to race, it is all about parameters—who sets them, who learns them, and who decides to operate within them. *In truth, we are not necessarily born black or white or red. We are born learning to be black or white or red.*

Chapter Seventeen

The Employee Paradox
Respecting the Psychology of Black Workmanship

In 1993, famed sociologist and University of California professor of Ethnic Studies Dr. Ronald Takaki wrote a spellbinding book entitled *A Different Mirror: A History of Multicultural America*. In his book, Takaki outlines several contextual arguments focusing on the complexities of diversity, culture, history, and geopolitics. The text is extremely well written, and although each of the constructs are of great interest, there is one specific ideal that seems to stand above the fray. I am referring to what Takaki calls the *master narrative*.

By and large, the term master narrative refers to the way the historical and cultural chronology of the United States has been conveyed from an oversimplified and culturally narrowed perspective. This perspective has been established specifically from the lips, minds, and ideals of white American men. This concept is not new. It has been discussed by many scholars and historians. None, however, does so more effectively than Takaki. Takaki explains how the master narrative attempts to reinforce the false belief that American progress (social, economic, and otherwise) has occurred solely as a direct byproduct of male Eurocentric grit and aptitude. The power of the master narrative lives primarily through a multitude of erroneous claims concerning what I like to call the three pillars framework: white-male diligence, white-male ingenuity, and white-male intelligence.

While it is true each pillar plays a prominent role in defining our nation's past, I find myself drawn to the power and presence of the first pillar: white-male diligence. By general definition, the concept of diligence refers to a man or woman's ability and/or propensity to carry out action, to work with haste, to be indefatigable, to strive toward a given objective regardless of challenges or obstacles. A diligent individual, all things being equal, is one who perseveres by way of his or her overt passion to get something done. American history is permeated with stories wherein white men have worked both diligently and passionately. The problem is not that these narratives exist. The problem is we are overwhelmed with such narratives. We have heard these narratives in preschool, elementary school, high school, and college. We have heard them on the news, the radio, and in books. This historical saturation has bogged down American history. More importantly, though, the saturation has cultivated a supremely false perception that white men in the United States have not only worked harder and faster to cultivate the American experiment than any other demographic. It also suggests white men have somehow cornered the historical market when it comes to occupational veracity, vocational prowess, and upward mobility. Add to this the prevalence of common archetypes and stereotypes, such as black laziness, for example, and the saturation becomes even more problematic. The white-male diligence pillar reinforces the idea that to be white and male is to come from a long line of hard workers and self-starters, almost suggesting hard work is a biological and/or genetic predisposition only analogous to non-black people. Hence the American fascination with white-male entrepreneurship, white-male ownership, the captains of industry, the robber barons, and various other bootstrap champions.

There is no real problem in giving white men their just due when it comes to their actual historical contributions. Individuals should be respected for their accomplishments, especially those who have positively impacted the growth of our nation. The problem occurs when acts of upward mobility and individual diligence are strictly and exclusively tied to the predilections of white men. The axiom of white-male diligence has been manipulated as a means to perpetuate the misconception that black men did not take part in the overall development of this so-called *grand experiment*, or that the role of women is somehow less important to the American zeitgeist. Black intellectualism assumes second fiddle to the ideological expressions of non-black seminal thinkers. You see, the goal of the master narrative is dualistic in nature. It promotes positive aspects of the white working paradigm while suppressing the legitimacy of black diligence.

Any historian worth his salt understands that without the blood, sweat, and tears of American black working people, this nation would cease to exist. There is no better way to push back against the falsehoods regarding the battle between black male ineptitude and white male diligence than to highlight the historical significance of black workers. One cannot discuss American progress, as it were, without asking, "What does it mean to be a black worker in modern day America?" This is an overtly challenging psychological inquiry because it is permeated with a multitude of moral cliffs and ethical valleys. To address this question, one must be open to historical and psychological excavation. One must be willing to dig deeper, with unabashed audacity, blasting downward through the blood-soaked sediment and tear-stained epochs of the North Atlantic slave trade, Jim and Jane Crow, the civil rights movement, and the postmodern struggle for black and brown economic freedom. For these are the spaces in which black truth rests its weary head—where black reality slumbers at the bottom of the rabbit hole. More importantly, to tussle with this question is to seek answers that fly directly in the face of the current American history.

As we begin to look closer at the experiences of black workers, we slowly uncover the psychological pain and stress they endure on a daily basis. We find the manner in which they push, with serious intent, to impress those who manage them, yet rarely understand them. The cultural disconnect is real. It is for this reason if we ask most black workers about their experiences on the job, industry notwithstanding, they will give us insight into a world only they can properly explain, where only they can feel the incessant cultural burn of American working life. Most will share, if asked, what it feels like to be consistently and overwhelmingly demotivated at work. Others will explain how it feels to be culturally misplaced. Some will allude to a feeling of being undervalued and underrepresented at the same time—to having succumbed to a plethora of cultural expectations. Others will, no doubt, speak of public stigmatization from their peers, thus hindering their ability to be productive and viable pieces of the collective puzzle. They will confide how it feels to work scared of being truthful or scared of succeeding and frightened of failure. Many are afraid of allowing their cultural truisms (those cultural behaviors and actions in which they feel comfortable) to shine through because they do not meld with acceptable behavioral standards of the whitewashed working world.

There is a level of complexity often overlooked concerning the black working experience. It is easy for some to forget the modern black worker is barely removed from slavery. It was only a few generations ago the modern black worker was a mere human mule transporting some substance from here to there, unable to raise his head proudly as he completed a given task. He was unable to throw his shoulders back and stiffen his neck with pride because his position in the American working world was relegated to servitude. The working conditions for black people have never been easy. Black employees are almost always looked at through a different lens with eyes that have a difficult time understanding the roles they are expected to play, the things they are to say and do. Black employees are expected to assimilate seamlessly with coworkers, especially those who are white and those who set the cultural tone for the American working world. In an attempt to cope, many black workers are expected to be their own cultural psychologists, self-diagnosing all the while as they work, keeping themselves in line and in check, talking inwardly, self-soothing, laughing at jokes that do not seem funny, and smiling when they would rather frown. Although academics and scholars alike often overlook the cognitive wound of black vocational fallout, the truth cannot be denied. *It is alive.* It is always breathing, always panting, gasping for air beneath the nation's historical loam, yet it is wedged between the temporal layers of now and then, still relevant to the moment. Despite the country's alleged ascent to post-racialism, the truth remains intact. *It is alive.*

Although there are countless ways we might classify or generalize the psychosocial circumstances that black employees have endured in response to their inauspicious introduction to the white working world, we must develop a clear connection in our minds that links the past with the present. This connection must do more than simply highlight the temporal work-related curve of black workers. It is important our discussion also provides a simplistic and recognizable framework that represents the current state of affairs; a framework worthy of further study that pushes back against these problems.

THE FOUR IDEALS MODEL

Before we delve into the details associated with the Four Ideals model, it is critical to point out that it is based on the perspectives of many black employees working within the United States and comes to us via reams of primary research. Altogether, this model suggests there are four critical motivational ideals representing the status quo for African-American employees. While it is true there are statistical outliers and there are those African American-workers who are motivated at work, research reminds us many black workers are demotivated and dissatisfied. For now, though, it is important to understand all four of the ideals are problematic realities. This is because, for one, they are overwhelmingly unknown and unrecognized by most American businesses. As a result, modern managers and corporate leaders have no real or proactive strategic approach to addressing the organizational fallout and lack of productivity created by the unmotivated black employee. Second, the ideals are problematic for modern organizations because they underscore the cultural disconnect that exists between black employees and non-black managers. Until we understand the psychocultural challenges presented by the aforementioned ideals, the cultural and managerial divide will continue to expand. Moreover, productivity and organizational unity will continue to decline. The four ideals, which are defined within the contextual framework of the model, include the misunderstood ideal, the misdiagnosed ideal, the misappropriated ideal, and the marginalized ideal.

The Misunderstood Ideal

Since there is a salient lack of research focusing on the psychological work lives of black employees, most organizations resort to making unfounded decisions regarding the black working community. Consequently, as a collective working demographic, many African-American employees find themselves working with and under managers who demonstrate little knowledge about black history, black culture, and black nuance. As a result, many black employees report they are misunderstood as a group. Being misunderstood as an employee is problematic for a multitude of reasons. White managers may, for example, assume black employees are not interested in moving up the proverbial corporate latter, which could lead to fewer promotions, pay raises, and company incentives. To misunderstand an employee, from a leadership point of view, is to increase the chances the employee remains dissatisfied with their work.

The Misdiagnosed Ideal

The lack of authentic and timely data concerning the psychology of black employees forces managers and leaders to guess at the best ways to motivate African-American workers. This lack of data leads to a misdiagnosis of sorts. The problem with guessing is most of these assumptions tend to be incorrect. An incorrect diagnosis is extremely costly in the modern business world because it wastes time and money. Another problem, one that is a bit more serious, is when black employees are assumed to act a certain way because of their race, there is a strong chance they will feel disrespected. Consequently, the misdiagnosed ideal leads to an unmotivated black workforce and a decline in operational productivity.

The Misappropriated Ideal

A large number of black employees report they feel as if they are being asked to work in capacities that do not align with their talent, cultural makeup, and/ or general skillset. In short, they feel they are doing the wrong tasks. The misappropriation of black workers is problematic because it ensures that black workers will never reach their full working potential. It also increases the chances the overall organization will experience a loss of operational productivity because it is not maximizing the talent of its black workforce. Displaced talent ensures employees are not being utilized to their full potential.

The Marginalized Ideal

To be misunderstood, misdiagnosed, and misappropriated as an employee is a challenge to say the least. There are those cases, however, where the challenge becomes even more problematic. In these instances, the lack of understanding regarding the employee's culture stands as a direct obstacle to the worker being hired in the first place, which is what has happened to a large number of African-American employees in the United States. We can see examples of this in data corresponding to black unemployment rates throughout the nation. This can also be seen in the data highlighting the large cross-section of black employees who are underemployed. Many black workers are marginalized and pushed aside in such a way that, particularly in specific professions, they are unlikely to be recruited or selected for the position. While it is difficult to motivate employees without understanding their cultural perspectives, it is impossible to motivate employees who were not hired in the first place.

The 4M Ideal is critical to understanding what it feels like to be a black worker. It is critical to ending the falsehoods related to white male diligence. It is critical to setting the record straight. It is critical to pushing back against the master narrative.

Chapter Eighteen

The Ascension of Desires Continuum

What Maslow Forgot to Tell You about Black Working People

In the previous essay, we tackled the historical interconnection between slavery and the modern black employee. It is one thing to discuss the complexities of the American black working life in relation to slavery. It is another thing altogether to juxtapose those historical realities with black employee motivation in the present day.

Abraham Maslow was a great man, but like any human being, the true greatness of his work must be examined in terms of both what he was and was not able to accomplish in his lifetime. To be sure, Maslow's work, particularly in the field of psychology, was more than noteworthy. He set a new standard regarding the understanding of the sociological complexities of motivation, self-actualization, and upward mobility. Yet, even as we recognize the power of his models and ideals, we must also point out the flaws connected to his theories. You see, there are areas of academic research that analyze the problematic defects regarding Maslow's hierarchy of needs model, but for the most part, the findings are relatively similar. It is vital we get past these rather common perspectives and look deeper. For when we get beyond the structural and foundational flaws, a much more important and overlooked issue bubbles to the surface. This issue, in a nutshell, is that Maslow's most recognizable motivation model, the hierarchy of needs theory, neglects to account for the cultural, racial, and ethnic nuances of black people.

Maslow's hierarchy model assumes all individuals are motivated not only in a relatively similar way but also that the cultural differences they demonstrate make no difference at all; race does not matter. This line of thinking represents an overly simplified and outdated modality where the assumption is all employees act, think, and see the world through the same cultural lens. Clearly, this is not the case. In light of current ideals intertwined with modern sociological theory as well as the obvious and trendy emphasis placed on promoting culturally diverse environments, the hierarchy of needs paradigm becomes less applicable by the minute.

A great deal has changed since the model was introduced, namely the ethnic makeup of American business entities and the realization that cultural realities tend to shape cognitive thought processes. Coming to terms with this point is one thing, doing something about it is another. With that thought in mind, I bring forward an evolutionary progression of the original model of Maslow's hierarchy of needs—a progression that fills in the gaping cracks and holes left by his previous models. I present the *ascension of desires continuum*. If properly implemented, this continuum can be used to help limit the spread of a construct I refer to as *culturemorbus* (the dangerous misconception that assumes all cultures think and act alike) and increase the motivation levels of countless African Americans in the United States.

It is not enough to identify the cultural and racial limitations associated with the hierarchy of needs model and its significant lack of focus on black nuance. Noticing the problem is only half of the battle. What is needed, as a means to complete the picture, is a well-developed solution to the dilemma—something that sets the record straight. We are talking primarily about a theoretical recalibration of sorts, one that aligns itself to fit the idiosyncratic gradations relevant to the specific socio-behavioral needs of black workers. This is clearly easier said than done because the solution, if it is to respect the work accomplished up to this point, must be constructed in such a way that it does not destroy or overshadow the foundational modality of Maslow's work. For even with its faults, the hierarchy of needs model is an extremely powerful and useful social tool. It can enhance the operational productivity of organizations and societies within and outside the United States, and it has been used in a myriad of settings.

As with all things under the sun, especially those things being recreated from a previous model, it is imperative a perceptive reexamination of names and labels take place. To be sure, names are powerful. More than symbolic gestures, names provide definitions and feelings—they quantify and clarify. With that in mind, let us begin the process by analyzing and reestablishing the names linked to Maslow's theory, beginning, of course, with the word hierarchy.

By general definition, a hierarchy is a structural configuration developed in such a way that it differentiates between what or who is located at its base as opposed to its top. It is a physical/tabular arrangement that provides meaning. Hierarchies are typically made up of a given array of items and/or levels. And so, as one thinks about social, educational, global, and governmental hierarchies, one surely envisions the structural formation associated with this term. It is easy to imagine the upper and lower regions of a given hierarchy.

It is also easy to imagine, as we stay with this point, the manner in which people tend to define themselves, depending on their position within a given hierarchy—grading each other based on position, labeling one another based on location in the pecking order. On the surface, the concept of a hierarchy may appear to be effective in that it supports the notion that motivation is analogous, primarily, to upward mobility. There is something about being human that makes us want to reach the top, to move upward. The problem with this wording, though, is it does not discuss the actions needed for one to make actual progress. It does not show us how to execute the motivational activities needed to move up the hierarchy. This is because one can have a strong understanding of what a hierarchy is but lack the necessary knowledge of how to climb that same hierarchy. What is needed, then, is an action word, a verb. A term steeped in movement that defines and demonstrates the physical and psychological energy it takes for black employees to experience inspiration from their jobs. For without movement, a hierarchy represents more of a barrier to achievement and upward mobility rather than a vehicle. Without movement, the hierarchy becomes a blockade when a ladder or a bridge would be more effective. Consequently, a new term must serve as a more suitable replacement for the term hierarchy. That term, dear reader, is ascension.

Ascension both equates to and promotes the spirit of mental and physical advancement—but not a typical or common type of advancement. It evokes a somewhat metaphysical imagery, a vision tied deeply to a person's divine spirituality and singular divinity. To ascend is to move upward, floating with grace, toward a place better and more important than that which remains below, to move beyond what is above.

To the layperson, the connection between ascension, employee motivation, and African-American culture may appear to be unrelated. Nothing, however, could be further from the truth. In reality, these constructs are inextricably intertwined. Rooted together like veins and capillaries, they bend and twist inside and atop one another. This is a connection Maslow could have uncovered had he expanded his theory to the cultural commonalities and social distinctions allied with the majority of black working people; the primary reason being, of course, that there are few racial groups existing in the United States more spiritual than black Americans. Black people, notwithstanding the way in which they are spread across the four corners of the American landscape, are highly religious folks. Spirituality and religion guide the way in which black people make most of their political and social decisions. It shapes their communities. In fact, a relatively recent study conducted by the world-renowned Brookings Institution stated black Americans, across the board, are the most religious demographic in the country. Another study conducted by the well-respected Pew Research Center reported of all American groups, blacks are more likely to claim membership of a given religious affiliation or spiritual organization. Black people are also less likely than any other American demographic to self-report as atheist or agnostic. Consequently, it would make sense for a motivation theory to be created to enhance the moral, spiritual, and organizational commitment of black workers and focus on helping black workers do more than just see or recognize a particular hierarchy from a business-related perspective. For this group, spirituality must be addressed. It must be tied to the process. Black workers have a desire to ascend, to become more than they are at the moment, and they have no inclination, as the research states, to check their spirituality at the door. In short, when it comes to black folk, no spiritual connection at work often translates to no motivation at work.

The second term in Maslow's model refers to needs. Maslow suggests motivation is highly predicated upon whether an individual's physiological, safety, social, esteem, and self-actualization needs are met. But as we delve into the contextual minutiae of what a need is, it becomes clear this term should also be replaced as it does not fit. Although Maslow was clearly ahead of the temporal curve when he first thought of using needs as his foundational denominator, the present world has moved well past the idea of meeting human needs, as has the black community. Such thoughts are now passé. Today, the name of the game is superseding needs, over-satisfying needs. We see manifestations of this in the ways our corporate entities push, often with reckless abandon, to create utility for customers across the board, making people feel as if they receive much more than they pay for. Since we are talking about modern black employees, those who live and work in a century replete with speedy information exchange, globalization, and a rapid proliferation of geo-global interconnectedness, the chosen term must coincide with the collective superseding of needs. It must represent the current psychographic reality of black modernity. Although there are quite a few terms that might fit the bill, none are as effective as desires. In contrast to the idea of a need, desire is a much more powerful construct. This is largely because the former takes a more expressive and innate form. It is more behavioral—more visceral, if you will. Desires are stronger. Desires are deeper. More importantly, though, they are a salient reflection of the hope that dwells in the hearts of African Americans. Also, desires fit the modern realities Americans reach for on a daily basis. The utilization of terms such as ascension and desires is a wonderful start, but they must be married to a specific ideological framework, hence the continuum.

As with many employee motivation and psychological motivation models, Maslow chose to classify his paradigm as a theory. By all accounts, a theory is a representation of a well-codified set of ideological suppositions based on a given belief or set of standards. While the use of the term theory is not a bad choice, a more suitable term would reiterate the need for black workers to reach higher levels of employee motivation and to mount up on wings as if motivation were a place that dwells only at the top, at the pinnacle. Maslow's approach suggests there is an endpoint to the motivation process. It posits as one progresses through each of the prescribed needs, he or she will eventually reach a place that stands as the final and ultimate phase of the individual's growth, a resting place of self-actualization. The problem with this line of thinking, especially as it relates to modern black workers, is motivation is hardly a resting place. It is a birthplace. Motivation has no prescribed end. It does not stop. It persists and endures, constantly escalating and swelling until the worker does more than become a part of their job. They become the job itself. While Maslow does an effective job of expressing the state of vocational euphoria one feels when they become self-actualized, he also assumes self-actualization is, in fact, the final stage of motivation.

For us to understand this point, we have to stretch our imaginations a bit. We have to grasp the idea that there are stages of motivation above and outside the self-actualization phase, unnamed stages most of us have yet to experience, that we are afraid to acknowledge because of the risk involved. If we allow ourselves to comprehend this idea, we quickly begin to realize the word theory, as Maslow uses it, does not do the model justice. For when we speak about employee motivation and the fact that it can be an infinite process, we also begin to understand we are talking about a continuum. A continuum is infinite. It keeps going on and on.

THE ASCENSION OF DESIRES CONTINUUM

The ascension of desires continuum is a specially designed employee motivation model created to meet the specific cultural and ethnic desires of African-American employees working in modern day America. It is the vocational and motivational response to culturemorbus. While the general formation of the model is based on the structural configuration of Maslow's hierarchy of needs theory, the ascension of desires continuum suggests the motivation of black workers includes meeting the desires of African-American employees, which include: black health desires, black safety desires, black collective desires, black psycho-efficacy desires, and black inner-cognizance desires. The following segments provide a brief overview of the desires.

Black Health Desires

The motivation of modern black employees cannot take place unless a clear and intentional effort is made to recognize the relationship between African-American culture and black mental/physical health. Doing so delays the ill effects of culturemorbus and ensures that motivation can manifest. This connection provides meaningful insight into a major cultural reality for black Americans across the board. Managers, organizational leaders, and change agents who assume they can motivate African-American employees without comprehending the myriad health risks black people live with on a daily basis are destined to fail. Unfortunately for black working people, specific types of health problems prove to be highly intergenerational. In addition, these health problems can serve as potential de-motivators, especially when the work environment is not conducive to black employees expressing their health-related frustrations and concerns. According to the Department of Health and Human Services and the Office of Minority Health, African Americans tend to post higher death rates than white Americans for stroke, cancer, pneumonia, homicide, HIV/AIDS, and diabetes. COVID-19 continues to decimate the black community, and black employees often don't have health insurance. In addition, based on the realization that mental health is also important, there is quite a bit of research regarding the mental health crisis affecting black workers. As reported by the Black Mental Health Alliance, African Americans make up close to 40 percent of homeless citizens, a large segment of whom suffer from depression, schizophrenia, anxiety, and bipolar disorder. There is a lack of mental health screening in the black community, and many of these mental health disorders are avoidable and/or treatable. It is critical that modern businesses and managers develop support systems for black employees who may be suffering from the aforementioned issues. The solutions these organizations utilize should be culturally specific, prevalent, and affordable.

Black Safety Desires

The motivation of modern black employees cannot take place unless a clear and intentional effort is made to recognize the relationship between black culture and black safety factors. Although circumstances are beginning to improve, a large percentage of black employees live in areas where general safety is threatened on a daily basis. To suggest this reality affects one's ability to be motivated at work is a clear understatement. It is also an understatement to suggest black poverty, the black working poor, and black safety are overtly intermingled. According to the Department of Health and Human Services and the Office of Minority Health, African Americans ranked lowest for household income, unemployment, homeownership, and insurance coverage. In addition, black Americans are more likely to commit and be victims of crimes such as rape, robbery, and aggravated assault. Not to mention the fact that police violence in the United States has become an epidemic in and of itself. Safety desires tend to be externalized quite differently in the minds of black workers because of the cultural realities involved. Modern organizations can not overlook these factors.

Black Collective Desires

Black employees tend to report that social camaraderie and teamwork play a critical role in the way they view work and employment. This has a great deal to do with the fact that black people, collectively, are an extremely social demographic. Black collective desires reinforce the manner in which black employees tend to rely on an atmosphere that allows for self-expression, openness, and frankness. This does not occur without a sense of employee unity. Organizations that limit the opportunities for black workers to communicate run the risk of negatively affecting black worker morale. They also increase the chances that black employees will limit their desire to be creative, innovative, and open to experience. Black collective desires can and must be adhered to because they not only enhance black employee motivation but also allow for black workers to feel connected to the corporation, the company culture, and the people they work with on a daily basis.

Black Psycho-Efficacy Desires

The term efficacy, in a general sense, refers to the capacity, the confidence, or the potential to reach a given point. By in large, self-efficacy is an individual's confidence that they can achieve a given objective. So, if a person demonstrates high levels of self-efficacy, they tend to be confident and assured in their own abilities. For black workers to ascend through the continuum, it is vital that modern organizations and managers cultivate work environments where black workers can work toward goals without obstacles or hindrances. For this to occur, black workers must be allowed to take part in the creation of their own work-related goals. They must also be given the leeway to change goals as they see fit, obtain the needed resources to reach goals, and be respected when they do reach these goals. More importantly, however, African-American employees should be given opportunities to follow and mentor other black workers. This is critical because it ensures that both the mentor and the mentee will have chances to reflect upon cultural commonalities and ways to cope with the various stressors of working in places that often overlook black realities.

Black Inner-Cognizance Desires

So much of what happens to us has to do with the way we see ourselves. While our perception of ourselves is important, it is also important we reach a level in our lives where we feel comfortable with the people we have become accustomed to being around. This is especially the case for black workers, many of whom report their respective work environments make them feel uncomfortable, misplaced, and overlooked. This is a problematic reality because, as has been supported by countless studies, motivation tends to occur when individuals are mentally relaxed. Black inner-cognizance refers to the way black workers think about themselves. Those who possess black inner-cognizance are not only proud and excited about their blackness, they are also in tune, emotionally and behaviorally, with the calm that comes with feeling secure. There are many ways companies can assist black workers in developing a sense of black inner-cognizance. They include, for example, championing the cultural values of black people, making them feel as if their blackness is a benefit to the company, placing black nuance on a pedestal, promoting workplace diversity initiatives, and remaining open to the differences those employees possess. This includes style of dress, musical choice, vernacular, acceptance of sexual orientation, and openness to forms of black self-expression. When modern business factions create atmospheres where black workers feel free to revel in their cultural center points, black employees will no longer feel the need to alter (or conceal) their cultural positions. Most importantly, they will experience the quiet calm that comes with knowing differences increase the validity and productivity of the workplace.

Chapter Nineteen

America's Dissociation Identity Disorder

Fearing the Blackness of Obama Part I

Many of us, when conversing via the customary discourse of the common moment, tend to stretch our arms hopelessly and helplessly toward a location of solemn quietness, especially when under duress. We succumb. We give up. We rest in the searing silence of a dark space, thus moving our emotional selves away from all that is allied with humanity, thereby running away. There are countless concepts and terms created to capture the spirit of such a desire. Some of these terms are contextual. Others appear, at least on their collective surfaces, to be a bit more colloquial in design. The most interesting of the lot, however, springs from the transformative zeitgeist of psychology and is known to most mental health professionals as dissociation. As we examine the rugged angles of this highly elusive term, we can recognize its multifarious duality. The term has a twoness to it, and when intimately scrutinized, the definition is both controversial and ironic. On one hand, it stresses the longing to move away. Yet on the other hand, it supports the notion of receding into oneself.

Our purpose, nevertheless, does not include paying much attention to the idiomatic manipulation of the concept. We are not interested in the slang-permeated verbiage that often accompanies dissociation because it is explicitly misleading. Moreover, it seems to dehumanize and deteriorate the truth of the concept. As a citizen of the world, you have heard it all before. I am positive you can recognize the street-level vernacular germane to dissociation: "I need to drop out and hide. This job is too demanding, and I never want to come back here." "I wish all these people would just leave me alone. I am so sick of hearing them talk." "The world would be a better place if everyone just got out of my way and left me alone." This type of wordage is not the dissociation we are speaking of, namely because it is not exactly psychological in nature. Besides, it lacks intellectual sincerity. Notwithstanding an individual's preoccupation with suicide, it is a lie to think people really want to be moved away from other people forever. Human beings, sociologically and otherwise, are created to be together, even when our divergent ideologies are at odds. We are born to communicate, partner, argue, quarrel, love, spit at, agree and disagree with one another, together even in hate. We can do nothing by ourselves. In fact, the entire premise of solitary confinement is based on the aforementioned truth. The most diabolical way to torture a human being does not necessarily encompass beatings, waterboarding, or sleep deprivation (though these are formidable tactics indeed), but placing someone in a dark box where he cannot argue and bicker with and adore and hate his brethren, which almost always seems to do the trick. This is most assuredly the case for other living animals as well and can be supported by the psychological work as seen in Harry Harlow's social isolation experiments with rhesus monkeys in the early 1960s.

In this essay, we are tackling a much more convoluted set of questions, questions which gnaw at the crux of psychological dissociation. For example, what happens to the individual who is emotionally incapable of monitoring their dissociative tendencies? How do they muddle through as their cognitive realities are eroded by a psychological rainstorm of torrential proportions, when their mind, and body for that matter, are nudged over a cliff, thus rendering them an excommunicated citizen of the world? How do they fight back against the current? What happens when the neurological modifications in their brain predetermine they are no longer the master of their fate and they do not get to choose when they *check out*? We are speaking of authentic dissociation—one that cannot be helped without the assistance of psychotherapy, hypnosis, and/or pharmacological interventions. We are speaking of a crushing personality dysfunction whereby the afflicted may experience fits of hysteria, social seclusion, paranoia, frustration, depression, and so on.

To be sure, the questions related to psychological dissociation are overtly intriguing, but we need to remember we have only examined the term as it relates to a particular individual. It would behoove us to study this expression in relation to practical events which have occurred throughout the modern United States. For example, we could examine the manner in which the American citizenry seems to be psychologically dissociated from learning for the simple sake of learning. We could, in addition, investigate the reasons why the ideological attitudes of young people in America are psychologically dissociated from the positions of older Americans. The idea being, of course, that younger folks operate under a unique cloak of unprecedented narcissism in direct opposition to socio-foundational ideals such as the protestant work ethic, for example. We could even, if we cared to venture forward, monitor the assorted economic stressors faced by those members of the country who are financially estranged from the so-called "American Dream." It is common knowledge that poor and rich Americans see the world differently, but the question is why? Each of these topics carries substantial merit and would lead to a lively debate of our tendency to dissociate ourselves.

All things being equal, I would like to consider this issue from a different vantage point, thus focusing on the peculiar yet overtly predictable circumstances which have occurred since the so-called transformative election of the first African-American President of the United States. To do this, we need to recall the psychological concept of dissociation is almost always conjoined with a major personality ailment referred to by many as dissociative identity disorder. While dissociation is attached to one's propensity to check out, dissociative identity disorder (DID) suggests some people, through no fault of their own, actually develop a multitude of separate and distinct personas. In other words, the original personality appears to splinter into a several disparate and inimitably dissimilar selves. Cognitively speaking, these people transmute into many other people, all living within the body of a single human being, sharing the same heart but operating in mental slivers.

Why is this important? Well, I submit for example that since the election of President Obama, the United States has succumbed to a full-blown case of certifiable and undeniable dissociative identity disorder. His recent election served as a psychological eruption, which violently shook the very underpinnings of what America was *supposed* to be. The act of electing a black man, one whose name evokes salient images of the Middle East and who also spent his early years as an inner-city community organizer, was groundbreaking. Yet after the dust settled, a year or two out of the gate, it became painfully clear the real fallout had just begun. The consequences were more race-based and psychological than anything else, hence the connection with DID. In fact, a cursory review of the current psychological literature plainly reports, among other things, that dissociative identity disorder tends to take root as the client fights to feel a homeostatic sense of self-protection and normalcy. In the battle to remain in control, the DID client innovates. He envisions several versions of himself to stand guard over his acutely bruised sense of inner-consciousness, prompted by those ravaging events that constitute his past.

A number of Americans are suffering from DID as a result of America's socio-cultural and political uneasiness with a black president, not to mention a good old-fashioned case of what I like to call *anti-afrotraitism* (the fear of black leadership). The historical roots of leadership theory postulates that leaders are, in fact, consecrated with a heritable mixture of genetic qualities which afford them the aptitude to enthuse followers by way of absolute intellect, educational prowess, and mental supremacy. This theoretical model is generally referred to as trait theory. As a result, history tends to link trait theory with the likes of Winston Churchill, FDR, John F. Kennedy, and various other non-black leaders. It is evident each of these men has demonstrated extraordinary leadership skills in his lifetime. Furthermore, this is not to suggest in any way that modern-day America has not embraced the global contributions of black and brown leaders. In addition to the fact that the trait model tends to genetically lionize white males, the problem is those black and brown leaders who stand as the favored few tend to be positioned in the segmented category of charismatic leaders as opposed to trait leaders. Whereas both models suggest traits are involved, charismatic traits tend to be more inspirational than inherently intelligent. Following what famed intellectual Max Weber often referred to as charismatic authority, these leaders possess an ability to elicit devotion in the hearts of those who listen, but they do so by way of dramatic showmanship. As socially valuable as charismatic leaders can be, we must acknowledge they are often given credit for their ability to connect with people and not so much for their intellectual prowess. A charismatic leader can create social change but does not necessarily have to demonstrate highly regarded mental faculties. It is for this reason black and brown icons such as Martin Luther King and Gandhi, for instance, are defined as having that indefinable something special. Whereas King's and Gandhi's accomplishments, from civil disobedience to Satyagraha, are historically irrefutable and deeply contextual, few theoretical models posit these traits were passed through the genealogical substructure associated with these men. There is a racist undertone in assuming such a stance namely because it hypothesizes that black and brown leaders are effective by way of their entertainment or charismatic skills as opposed to what is in their minds. This is an old and well-documented argument. It brings to mind, of course, the turbulent, visceral, and hackneyed subjugation of black people in the media ranging from "stepinfetchit" to modern day Hollywood "coonery." It is true that an explosion of new leadership theories has weakened the acceptance of the trait approach, but the model remains alive and well in many corners of American culture.

A principal predicament has surfaced in America, one that has stunted the former president's ability to win ethical hearts and moral minds. The predicament is that many Americans exude a discomfort with black leaders. It is very difficult for many non-black citizens to recognize President Obama is a natural born leader because to do so, one would have to also agree that the president is genetically linked to generations of people carrying his leadership traits. This would include dismissing many of the age-old myths so often associated with black Americans and succumbing to the notion that black intellectualism is not inferior. Moreover, it would support the idea that the achievement gap is based on sociological circumstances, black self-determinism is inhibited by the nation's socioeconomic environment, affirmative action is a necessary tool even in today's modernized America, and Herbert Spencer's social Darwinism must be reexamined in regard to people of color. To agree with each of the aforementioned paradigms, for some Americans, is simply asking too much. Despite the many Americans who have no problem doing so, a large demographic refuses to take part in avant-garde ideologies regarding race, hence the affiliation with anti-afrotraitism.

Anti-afrotraitism is, for one, a sociological paradigm signifying the beliefs espoused by some Americans that people of color are genetically incapable of leading non-blacks in an effective manner. This is hardly a new phenomenon. In fact, several blacks were elected to Congress in the 1800s as a result of the congressional reconstruction acts. Since certain southern states were predominantly black, it is not surprising that states such as Louisiana and South Carolina elected black government officials to serve in the United States government. As these former slaves and self-educated black men took office, they were immediately affected by *anti-afrotraitism*. It did not matter some spoke several languages in a time when most men could not read. It did not matter some proposed political positions that could have enhanced the economic growth for both black and white Americans. Some were elected but never seated, some were forced to serve shorter terms, and some were displaced by way of fraudulent voting tactics. Regardless of the outcome, it was clear America was not ready to follow the lead of black representatives nor was it prepared to recognize the intellectual capabilities of those men. One could also guess, in keeping with this era, many Southern countrymen would have disagreed that black governmental leaders acquired their leadership skills from the genetic traits of previous slaves.

Even today, as modern history books are overflowing with the wisdom of John Jay, John Adams, and Alexander Hamilton, little is discussed about the early black congressmen. We permeate the minds of our American children with the accounts of the Revolution but omit the life of Robert De Large, the African-American man who represented South Carolina in the 1870s. We venerate the intelligence of Benjamin Franklin but overlook Alonzo Ransier, the black congressmen elected in Georgia in 1872. Who is telling the stories of Jefferson Franklin Long from Georgia, Robert Elliott from South Carolina, or James Rapier from Alabama? For these stories are obscured under the buckling weight of historical revisionism, institutional racism, and a good old-fashioned dose of *anti-afrotraitism*.

We must clarify here that many racist Americans, those who disagree specifically with the political advancement of black government officials, have no problem with black leaders leading black people. In fact, they often cherry-pick unconnected and overused examples when black political leaders failed in their attempt to lead predominately black cities. Examples include former D.C. Mayor Marion Barry, who was filmed in a hotel room using crack cocaine, Baltimore Mayor Sheila Dixon, who was accused for misappropriation of funds, and former Detroit Mayor Kwame Kilpatrick, who was ousted for an improper relationship with his female chief of staff. I find it a bit humorous that the names Scooter Libby, Mark Sanford, and Rod Blagojevich are omitted from the discussion.

The problem for anti-afrotraitism surfaces when these same black leaders, even those democratically elected by a myriad of races, attempt to lead white Americans. Anti-afrotraitism is also a term that rails against the idea that black and brown people could ever be natural born leaders. We are unmistakably talking here about two types of people. The former would be those who are culturally and racially progressive, and the latter would be those who are culturally and racially digressive. For the digressive demographic, Obama's presence is a psychological and painful reality. I mean, let's get real; it must be unequivocally shocking to digressive America to see what change has brought. It must be alarming for some to juxtapose the blackness of Obama with the whiteness of the nation's most distinguished founders including Jefferson, Adams, and so on. Or to see Obama's presidential portrait lined up on suburban school classroom posters amongst his peers, his skin iridescent in bronze amid the pale backdrop. For the digressive, it must be peculiar to imagine the president ambling through the White House encircled by the ghosts of slaves who once served as lay builders and waitstaff, watching him as he casts pronouncements regarding the very well-being of our homeland. It must be conspicuously bizarre to envision the fullness of the first lady's ethnic lips and the South Side Chicago swagger in her hips as she saunters through the nation's first garden, planting seeds for future first ladies to water. To see the president's coffee-skinned offspring, skinny and smiling, skipping down the hallway once closed to people of their ethnicity. Obama's blackness, despite the fact he is actually biracial, has created an intra-cognitive chain reaction for many digressive Americans. To cope with this extraordinary mental upheaval, Americans have erected a recipe of reactionary alter egos, if you will.

There is a Freudian construct called cathexis, which refers to the kinetic intellectual energy that lies dormant in people, dwelling under the surface and waiting to be liberated. The most assured way to prompt the release of what lies beneath the psychological surface, one must be questioned and goaded to divulge. Alas, more questions arise. What veracities do we unearth as we slip on our mental health hats and proceed to place the collective country on the therapist's couch? What is uncovered as we confidently pepper our emblematic client of red, white, and blue with an introspective barrage of Socratic queries? What happens when we pose the following question: "What is happening in today's America?"

It is my belief that we find, securely threaded into the locks of the American scalp, specific and stress-induced dissociative personality typologies, all of which agree on one specific thing. They all concur, with conviction, that no matter what Obama did or did not do, they would never have given him their full support. They would never stand by his ideas or agree with his decisions—not as a human being, not as black intellectual, and most certainly not as the leader of the free world. For these specific groups, Obama's race is an impenetrable wall that disallows them to place their trust in the elected leader of their beloved nation. This separation is monumental because it has forced pro-American non-black citizens to turn their collective backs on the one who has been chosen to defend and lead them. To comprehend the power associated with each of the American DID personalities, we need to jump headfirst into each. We need to find out their names. We need to know what makes them tick. In the spirit of such a journey and under the guise of therapeutic intervention, let us begin with the first Obama-inspired American personality/identity. Let's begin with Judd.

As the psychoanalysis session begins, we grab our notepad, slide to the front of our chair, and ask our client of America, "To whom am I speaking at this moment?" After a brief hush, we observe closely as the client sits erect on the couch, shifting his weight forward, nervously rubbing his hands on his knees. The physical transformation has begun, yet a silence ensues. In an attempt to prompt a response, we ask again in a more cogent manner, "To whom am I speaking now?" The previous silence breaks like a shattered window as the client's nervous voice utters, "I'm Judd. How many times are you gonna ask me that?"

As the session continues, we find out that Judd is a forty-something Caucasian-American, living in the corn-permeated flatlands of Middle America. He worked in a manufacturing plant for eighteen years, pressing metal and boxing electrical parts for microwave ovens. Judd's father and his father's father worked in that same plant, walking those same dust bowl roads to work, and dwelling in the same family home. He lives with his wife and is the father of three teenage girls, one of whom is three months pregnant. He informs us, with a bit of an attitude, he was laid off from his job six months prior to our conversation and holds a high school diploma from West Franklin High School. He was the backup quarterback, married his high school sweetheart, and did a stint in the first Gulf War.

Still digging, we ask Judd about his happiness, or lack thereof. "Are you a happy person, Judd?" His blank stare curls into an edgy smile. As he hears the question, we watch Judd's eyes glaze over. His head drops, and again his hands nervously rub his knees. "Judd," we ask, "What's happening in today's America?"

A bright light replaces the aforementioned blankness. A sense of energy takes over. "This country is going to hell," he sputters.

"Why do you say that?" we query. Wincing as though he stubbed his toe, he unleashes a verbal tirade. "We don't know what the hell we are doing anymore. We have made ourselves look weak from a military point of view, ya know? We need to put more time and money into protecting our citizens instead of just, ya know, taking care of the poor and giving a bunch of handouts."

"Is that what we are doing?" we fire back.

Again, the tirade takes shape. "Hell, yes! The damn president is just doing all this communist stuff, ya' know. He's giving money to the big companies and trying to make sure that we lose our jobs. I ain't worked in a long time over this crap. I am sorry. I just don't like him. I don't like Obama. It's embarrassing we got this guy up there in the White House. He is uppity, ya know? The guy acts like he knows everything up there. He's being arrogant and sayin' that we need to change the way this country works. Change it for what? It's just fine the way it is. He's a smooth-talkin' car salesman. That's all he is. And he's apologizing all the time for the country and . . . well, we just need to go back to the old America . . . go back to the way it used to be."

None of the perspectives demonstrated in Judd's dissociative harangue is surprising. Some might attest they are, in fact, a cultural manifestation learned from the habitat into which Judd was born or what Freud might refer to as Judd's *archaic heritage*. In this case, we are speaking of the remnants of ripened generational ideology leftover from the spoils of the Civil War, Confederate flags, and Jim Crow. It is also not surprising Judd's worldview shapes his conclusions concerning the nation's ostensible deterioration as a world power or America's hypothetical proclivity to appease its enemies. These tend to be conservative positions, each of which is arguable to say the least. Nor is it astonishing that Judd is embarrassed by the emblematic imagery of the current president. That Judd thinks Obama is supercilious and uppity is even more interesting, namely because it hearkens back to the antebellum epoch. History has well documented the relationship between the words *uppity* and *black*. It is critical to point out, for example, that slaves who learned to read did not only go against the laws of the day. They were also considered to be uppity. In fact, any and all forms of edifying self-determinism by black slaves were associated with being socially pretentious and culturally pompous. Slaves were expected to recoil in public, smile when nothing was funny, and follow the rules as determined by the master. Allowing a slave to read was antithetical to ensuring he developed a sense of self-efficacy, so these tactics were used as primal forms of psychological combat. Controlling the mind was a much more effective means of social incarceration than whipping, beating, and killing.

This brings to mind the foundational notions of infamous slave owner Willy Lynch, who taught slave masters to rely on a psycho-emotional stratagem as a means of controlling slaves. The objective was not so much to focus on physical control but to pit slaves against one another, to manipulate the slaves' confidence, and to reduce their desire to be educated. Lynch suggested slaves be separated by way of complexion, thereby constituting a caste system which placed dark-skinned blacks at the bottom of the hierarchy. Such actions would propel the slave into an unwinnable battle against himself and shift the struggle for power away from the master. It is important to point out the controversial nature regarding the authenticity of Lynch's teachings. While some historical accounts solidify his points, others refute Lynch's very existence. In looking at the horrid realities of slavery, it does not seem surprising such actions were taken.

Thousands of racially progressive-thinking whites and blacks, both liberal and conservative, have overcome the so-called Willie Lynch mentality. They recognize the importance of diversity and the remarkable accomplishment of selecting Obama as the President of the United States. There are also many who did not vote for the president who would not qualify as racist. That, along with reams of research literature sighting the statistical correlation between diverse communities and productive outcomes, a large part of America has realized the economic importance of cultural synergy. America is much better for it. This is indeed a wonderful thing. But let's not deceive ourselves. There is another contingent lurking throughout the American landscape. This contingent perceives Obama's intellectual elegance and ethnic confidence as nothing more than *black uppityness*. I call those who fall into this rather interesting category *Afro-trepidationist.* These are people, as the coined term denotes, who fear the educational progress of black Americans primarily because it allows for black individuals to engender modifications in the cultural power dynamics of the country. It is commonly known in the modern epoch, knowledge is analogous to power. If this is true, then African Americans who demonstrate knowledge become more powerful. This power is often recognized, by some, as conceit. In some respects, Afro-trepidationists are analogous to what is commonly referred to as *anti-intellectuals*, suggesting those who survive by way of knowledge acquisition rely too much on theory, social research, and various other pedagogical ideals. To be an anti-intellectual is to follow the populist, ordinary-man ideal as opposed to the affected instructions of the so-called academic elite. Where the two concepts differ, though, is that Afro-trepidationists have an apparent bête noire for black intellectuals.

They postulate that black intellectuals utilize their erudition to dismantle the cultural status quo in America, stripping the country of its original ideals, ripping it from the clutches of the common man. This is of particular importance for Judd as it ties to the last sentiment in his tirade. Judd rails against the black president's desire to interrupt the status quo. To Judd, Obama's desire to change the political game plan will, at some point, turn America on its proverbial head. After all, why wouldn't this black man with the African name and the Ivy League education want to change the way America works? Accordingly, Judd insists the key to true political and cultural salvation includes "going back to the way the world used to be," for this is a theme that has overtaken the anti-Obama movement with a furious tenacity and is a dominant theme for a large cross-section of the United States.

It is one thing to fear change. Research strongly supports the somewhat inherent need human beings possess to maintain the status quo. It is another thing, however, to fear black change specifically; to fear the shift in the racial pendulum of power, education and success, as it relates to black people. In recognition of this type of thinking, especially for those mirroring Judd's dissociative persona, it is vital we challenge such a notion. In other words, what does it mean to suggest we should go back to "the way things used to be?" What are we saying when we ask for the days of yesteryear or when members of the anti-Obama tea party brigades display signs at their rallies linking Obama to Adolf Hitler? More importantly, how far back do we want to go? Shall we go back to the time of the first presidency, the original administration of George Washington? Doing so would include transporting us to a period when a myriad of positive events took place, at least from a military/governmental perspective. It was during this period that the Continental Congress named Washington to the country's highest office; it was the time when Washington crossed the Delaware with a rag-tag militia and managed to send a crushing blow the British, thus securing American independence. It was a time when the nation dug its heels into the fertile ground and founded this political experiment we call the United States of America—all important events, to be sure.

In recognition of the importance of these historical activities, however, let us not forget the state of life for black people when Washington was in office. Let's not omit the fact that Washington, the nation's first chief executive, was not elected democratically. He was appointed by Congress, which seems to be a bit anti-American on its face, and black people played no part in the selection of our nation's first president. Let us not overlook the fact that Washington owned hundreds of slaves and black people were considered chattel, working the president's farms and living an animalistic existence under the weight of that peculiar institution. Is that what Judd is talking about? Is this far enough back? Maybe Judd would like the system to regress to the days of Jim and Jane Crow, the fight for suffrage, church bombings, ERA, etc. Maybe Judd would like to re-visit the 1950s when schools, lunch counters, and swimming pools were segregated.

Judd's bouts with Afro-traitism and Afro-trepidationism leave him with little recourse. He is cornered. As an American citizen, he must accept the choice for president has been made. On the other hand, he must also acknowledge the leader of his beloved country is an African-American intellectual with a progressive political agenda. Despite these points, Judd's persona does not allow him to give up without a fight, so he attempts to argue against the legitimacy of Obama's presidency. If he can disprove the president's authenticity, then his dissociative perspectives will stand. He claims, for example, Obama is not an actual citizen of the nation, suggesting the president's birth certificate is a fake. When this fails, he claims that president's oath of office was improperly conducted, meaning the president is unlawfully holding his seat. When this is brushed aside, Judd attempts to cast Obama as a radical outcast who shares ideological connections with hate mongers and anti-Americans. When this is dispelled, Judd claims the president is a global court jester, he is hardly a man mentally equipped for the job at hand, and he has no substance. Again, these notions are brushed aside. When President Obama is awarded the Nobel Peace Prize, Judd asserts Obama is not worthy of the award. Judd is not enraged, however, when De Klerk received the award, despite the former South African prime minister's long history of supporting apartheid policies, racial caste systems, and educational segregation. Judd does not refute the Nobel Prize given to Henry Kissinger, the former U.S. secretary of state who was involved in the clandestine bombing of Cambodia and the prompting of the Pol Pot killings.

As Judd's cerebral disposition begins to wither into the client's inner consciousness, another of the various identities begins to initiate activation. It both gradually and increasingly bubbles to the emotional surface, bombarding it all the way through the mental birth canal, pushing and thrusting until it supersedes Judd's neo-conservative revelations. In what seems an instant, Judd is gone.

Recognizing the apparent shift in neuroses, the therapist steadies himself and launches the familiar starting question.

"To whom am I talking to now?"

This new personality allows his torso to slither down into the contours of the couch as he places both hands comfortably behind his head. His legs are straight and extended, and his feet are crossed. He looks as if he is both comfortable and uncomfortable—as if he is gloomy and joyful, proud and mortified.

Watching the human dichotomy who sits before him, the therapist listens as the patient speaks.

"What's up?" he asks. "I'm Jamal. Who are you?"

In as professional a tone as possible, the therapist explains the rules of the game and encourages Jamal to speak freely. Jamal complies, reminding the therapist he is never afraid to speak his mind.

"What is happening in this country, Jamal?"

Jamal's response is long-winded, yet coolly disseminated. "Man, there are so many things wrong wit' dis' country that I don't even know where to start."

"Well," the therapist responds, "Let's start with the current president. How is he doing?" Jamal rolls his eyes and pushes the air from his lungs.

"I gotta be honest witchu man, I am happy that a black man is in the White House, but I ain't really expectin' him to do much. Hell, he ain't nothin' but an opportunist, anyway. He is white when they want him to be white and black when we want him to be black. Yeah, he's smart and whatnot, but he ain't moving fast enough for me. Come on man, he done been in office for a year now, and he still ain't really done nothin' for black people. He ain't fixed the ghettos; the schools still suck. He ain't really changed all that stuff he said he was gonna change. I think he needs to do more stuff at a faster rate, ya' dig? I'm sorry, but I just ain't impressed."

Jamal's position, ironically, is much more in line with Judd's than one might realize. Both identities are skeptical, yet the origin of the skepticism resonates from two distinctly different places. Judd's fears are not only self-absorbed but also paranoid in that he assumes that Obama is out to get him, to harm him and all those who look and think as he does, or to change his pseudo-comfortable white Midwestern way of living. He forgets Obama shares many of these same values. He overlooks the fact that Obama is more pragmatic than radical, more even-tempered than reactionary, and just as much white as he is black. He forgets that Obama has family roots tied to Kansas and a white grandfather who served in the war. All of these truths are covered by the president's blackness.

In contrast with Judd, Jamal's skepticism is permeated with an ironic form of protective pessimism. He is not challenging Obama's ability or desire to correct the country's ills. He is unsure if the president will be allowed to do so in light of the current racial and political climate in the United States. It is as if he is afraid to confess he actually wants Obama to succeed, so he lessens the stakes by bringing up the various segments of the country that are still suffering by harping on what has not changed under any of the previous administrations, locked into a state of what Freud called *endopsychic conflict*. He is confused as to what he wants to happen and what will actually happen. Maybe he recognizes the fact that Obama's election can only fractionally alter the racial circumstances in this country. Maybe he recognizes that when Obama became president, the Senate once again became 100 percent white. Maybe he recognizes even the power residing in the leader of the free world cannot change the mindset of a single racist individual. With that, Jamal begins his statements by recognizing the historical influence of the Obama phenomenon. It is as if he feels obligated, by skin tone, to pay homage to Obama's accomplishments. Yet directly after the compliments, he holds the first black president accountable for solutions that have been omitted by almost every president to date. He overlooks the fact that ghetto poverty, for example, is an American mainstay, one that dates back long before the age of Obama. While he clearly recognizes the man's intelligence, Jamal is angry that Obama has not done more for black and brown people. So, on one hand, Obama must attempt to meet the conservative needs of Judd while simultaneously catering to the black progressive desires of Jamal. He must be ultra-conservative and super-liberal at the same time. He must be radically black and pragmatically white at the same time. No other president in the history of this country has been confronted with such a dilemma. None have had to walk such a tightrope whereby white Americans fear his blackness and black Americans fear his solidarity to non-blacks. All the while, there are even more identities to deal with.

As the conversation builds, Jamal disappears only to be replaced by a new character, this one a highly educated woman from New York named Louisa. She bursts onto the scene with undaunted bravado, interrupting the therapist before he can even begin.

"Look, I've already heard the questions," she boasts. "I totally disagree with those other two idiots to whom you were speaking." Her words are rapid as she continues, "My problem is not with Obama per se; I mean, he does have a few things on the table that are positive, but I think that he is pandering to the male establishment."

"What do you mean?" the therapist counters.

Louisa wets her lips and tosses her hair as if trying to remove it from her eyes. "Look, the United States is dominated by male superiority. Men make more than females in every industry, the government is flooded with men, and Obama cannot help but continue this trend. He, himself, is a man, and why should it be any different? Just because he is black? We should have elected Hillary. She would have brought a tough sensitivity we have never seen in this country. She would have been able to lead like a woman."

Next, Louisa presents yet another obstacle for the president. "Despite breaking down the obvious racial and ethnic barriers, Obama's presidential masculinity remains in line with the historical pedigree of this country. His maleness will surely affect his decisions regarding military policy, international trade, immigration, and the like."

What Louisa disregards, nonetheless, is Obama tends to stress the need for empathy. This is critical since empathy tends to be universally seen as a feminine trait. The president speaks of it rather frequently. In fact, empathy played a major role in a landmark decision to do what no other president has ever accomplished since the inception of this great nation. Obama selected a Latina woman to serve as the next associate justice of the Supreme Court. His efforts did not stop with the choice of Sotomayor; Obama has also created several governmental commissions focusing on female empowerment. The most obvious of these formations is the Council for the Advancement of Women and Girls, headed by White House staffer Valerie Jarrett. The council has pledged to focus on fair pay, childcare support, reducing economic disparities for women, etc. Moreover, the president signed into law the groundbreaking Lilly Ledbetter Fair Pay Act. These efforts notwithstanding, Obama will continue to have trouble garnering the support of some feminists simply because of his maleness. It is important to point out, as we discuss the president's maleness, his gender carries special connotations because it is intermingled with his blackness. Black men, for a host of reasons, are seen in a different light than their white counterparts. Black male anger, for example, is presented differently from white male anger on television, radio, and various other media outlets. The recent tea parties held primarily by white right-wingers are often looked at as peaceful means to make a political point. Conversely, black men standing in unison against the government for the reaction to Katrina are seen as a potentially violent expression of unruly civil aggression. This remains the case across the board. So the challenge produces more thorns. Obama is expected to meet the needs of Judd and his conservative ideals, Jamal and his progressive notions, and Louisa's desire for a more feminist agenda.

As Louisa subsides into nothingness, the therapist can see the exhaustion in the client's eyes. The transformation from one psycho-identity to the next seems to have taken its toll. Although the aura in the room suggests the session is about to end, a final personality emerges from the shadows. His name is Jason.

"What about me?" he screams, spraying saliva across the room and glaring through deeply dilated pupils. "People are always trying to leave me out of the discussion," he blasts.

The therapist, remaining calm, informs Jason he had no intention of leaving him out and asks him what he thinks about the current state of the American system.

Jason eagerly begins, "I don't know that much about it to tell you the truth. I am just eighteen, and me and my friends, right . . . well, we just don't think all that political stuff even matters."

"Why not?" the therapist asks.

"Well, it's just that that Obama guy is only going to be in office for a while and then some other guy will get in. It's not like it matters. Besides, the president doesn't have much power, anyway. He can't change stuff by himself. He doesn't even make much money. It's all joke, ya know?"

Listening to Jason, one comes to grips with the overwhelming sense of his political nihilism. It is easy to see his overall lack of interest, not just in the office of the president but in the American system as it stands. There does not seem to be a dislike or distrust for Obama per se. There is a lack of trust in the system, couched in the ignorant misjudgment of the president's power. To Jason, power is analogous to financial standing, not the oval office. This is highly problematic in that Jason does not realize the president has enormous amounts of power. Obama can veto legislation he does not agree with; he can use the proverbial bully pulpit to push his political agenda; he can make, promote, or not promote war; he can select judges who shape the legal/constitutional guidelines regarding abortion, same sex marriage, juvenile capital punishment, and habeas corpus—the list goes on.

At the writing of this piece, Obama's approval rating hovers around fifty percent, which, when juxtaposed with previous administrations, is relatively high. I point this out to remind the reader there are those who agree with the president's decisions. To be sure, this group consists of countless racial, cultural, and socioeconomic psychographics. As the pressure continues to mount and the country continues to work through its issues of race, we can be sure America's bout with DID will only increase. More identities will surface, and more fears will ensure Obama's challenges will remain great. This point notwithstanding, the president has my full support. Accordingly, I will stand in line with him as the elected leader of my beloved country, the military leader of the most powerful armed forces in the world, and as a powerful black intellectual.

Chapter Twenty

America's Dissociation Identity Disorder

Fearing the Blackness of Obama Part II: Trapped in the Throes of White Narcissism

So, here we are, eight years post Obama. Although his Presidency was far from perfect, the evidence suggests the Obama era was quite monumental. In addition to changing the political landscape as it relates to racial imagery and cultural symbolism, the Obama team managed to pass a healthcare reform bill that provided health insurance for over twenty million people and eliminated issues regarding preexisting conditions. He signed an economic recovery bill into law, which added millions of new jobs. He halted what was, at that time, the worst economic depression in the United States since the Great Depression and signed the Dodd-Frank Act into law, which pushed back against corporate fraud. Obama brokered a deal to halt Iran's nuclear capabilities, ordered the special forces raid that eventually killed Osama Bin Laden, repealed "Don't Ask, Don't Tell," and set new guidelines limiting carbon emissions. He protected the Dreamers from deportation, cultivated a culture of net neutrality, and nominated the first Hispanic woman to the Supreme Court. Under the Obama administration, funding for Veterans Affairs was dramatically increased, embryotic stem cell research was enhanced, the Freedom of Information Act was emboldened, more stringent requirements for lobbyists were created, the salaries of senior White House officials were reduced, and unemployment benefits were enhanced. Not only did Obama order all American troops be pulled out of Iraq in 2011, he signed the Healthy, Hunger-Free Kids Act into law to improved school lunch programs, he increased the overall budget of the Food and Drug Administration, expanded the CHIP program (Children's Health Insurance Program), signed an executive order protecting members of the LGBTQ community from discrimination in the workplace, and forced Syria to destroy its stockpile of chemical weapons . . . and, oh yeah, he won the Nobel Peace Prize.

In the previous essay, we discussed the notion that the United States, figuratively speaking, suffers from dissociative identity disorder. The essay provided metaphorical examples, but it was to be taken primarily as a tongue-in-cheek valuation of the nation's disparate psychological reactions to the election of Barack Obama. As I scan the current political landscape, heading into the final months of Trump's first term, I am overwhelmed by the irony. Eight years ago, I suggested the nation was suffering from a mental disorder. Today, however, I am watching the nation being led by a leader who appears to be suffering from an actual and real mental health disorder. No metaphors. No symbolism or tongue-in-cheek allegory. President Trump carries himself as a man suffering from a clear case of narcissistic personality disorder. As a social scientist, I find the psychological state of President Trump fascinating, to say the least. But what is even more fascinating, and scary for that matter, is watching the socio-political fallout directly associated with his narcissistic actions.

Before we delve into the particulars as they relate to Trump's actions, let us first review narcissistic personality disorder. Surprisingly, NPD is much more common than many people realize. Over three million people a year are diagnosed with the disorder. Even more surprising is the fact that a large percentage of those three million people are directed to seek professional support from medical professionals. The primary tenants of NPD include an ostentatious sense of self-importance partnered with an inability to demonstrate empathy. Narcissistic people not only spend a great deal of time seeking admiration from others, they can also be extremely haughty, entitled, and arrogant. The problem with narcissistic behavior, among other things, is it oftentimes takes the forms of belittling others, bullying, and exaggerating accomplishments. Any psychoanalyst worth their salt would be able to see Trump demonstrates these behaviors daily, either through his tweets, speeches, or public interviews. What makes Trump's behaviors so impactful, however, is they are intermingled with a deep lack of understanding about a wealth of political topics. One would imagine, also, Trump is quite limited from an emotional intelligence and social intelligence point of view. It is important I add that there is another form of NPD called malignant narcissism, which is much more dangerous. The malignant version may be more suitable as it relates to Trump primarily because it is linked with sociopathy, paranoia, sadism, and distrust.

At the writing of this essay, the country finds itself in the midst of one its darkest epochs. America is currently trapped within the deadly confines of a global pandemic (COVID-19) in which 145,000 American citizens have died. Most sources report black folks are three times as likely to die from

COVID-19 as opposed to white Americans. Moreover, white Americans and Asian Americans report the lowest rates for COVID-19.

The government has been flailing in its response, and the Trump administration is being blamed quite frequently for its lackluster reaction to the virus. Political controversies are arising daily with regards to the opening/reopening of states, legislation regarding the usage of masks, school closures, and the notion Trump is not taking the virus seriously.

In addition to the fallout caused by the virus, the nation has been exposed to countless riots and demonstrations in every major American city in response to the death of an unarmed black man named George Floyd. A video of Floyd's death was shared on social media. Floyd was murdered by a group of Minneapolis police officers. The lead officer, Derik Chauvin, remains in custody at the time of this writing for kneeling on Floyd's neck for upwards of eight minutes, despite the fact that Floyd was pleading for his life and claiming he could not breathe. The Floyd case, in line with countless other similar cases (Adama Traoré, Freddie Gray, Sam DuBose, Philando Castile, Terence Crutcher, Walter Scott, Eric Harris, Tamir Rice) cultivated a visceral reaction from the broader American citizenry.

One of the most interesting surprises linked to the Floyd case has to do with the general reaction of white Americans. By in large, white Americans have been extremely supportive of the Black Lives Matter movement. The Trump administration, as a result, has found itself fighting against a diverse racial/ethnic coalition of American citizens primed on seeing changes in police brutality laws across the board. Trump's rhetoric seems to stand in direct contrast with those supporting Floyd, thus adding fuel to the political fire.

As if the global pandemic and police brutality issues are not enough, Trump's various other presidential failures have included tax breaks for the wealthiest of Americans, drastic budgetary cuts to social security, a demonization of immigrants, strange relationships with Russian oligarchs, a widening of the gap between rich and poor, a bottoming out of the consumer confidence index, and a decrease in humanitarian aid overseas. At the time of this writing, over thirty-seven million Americans applied for unemployment during the past four months, and the current unemployment rate stands at close to fifteen percent. For black folks in the United States, the current unemployment rate is currently close to seventeen percent. To put things in perspective, the unemployment rate during Great Depression tallied between seventeen percent and twenty-five percent.

While the current economy is cratering under Trump, it is clear he has been on the defensive. His defensiveness is what allows one to clearly see his narcissistic disorder in full bloom. Even a cursory review of Trump's actions, beginning during his campaign, highlights his proclivity to lack empathy and bully those who question him. Trump has, for instance, claimed publicly that he is the most popular person in Europe; publicly referred to his ex-girlfriend, porn star Stormy Daniels, as "horse face;" claimed he has the constitutional right to pardon himself; referred to nations such as Haiti and Nigeria as "shithole countries;" bragged about groping women in an interview on Access Hollywood; attempted to embarrass a Gold Star mother regarding her nationality and cultural customs; claimed dodging taxes made him smart; publicly called for Russia to hack the emails of a presidential candidate; attacked the ethnicity of a Mexican judge overseeing a fraud case focusing on the now defunct Trump University; claimed the late John McCain was not, in fact, a war hero because he got caught; publicly mocked a woman with a disability during a campaign speech; and claimed he could stand in the middle of New York and shoot someone and still be supported by the voting public. As we head to the next election, we will see if narcissism rules the day. Time will tell.

Chapter Twenty-One

A Morning on Poplar Grove

Early rise as a sultry sun eases along a dotted city skyline
uncoil and stretch
while my boyish legs dangle
and untangle
onto a nail-infested hardwood floor.
Breakfast scents glide up crooked and curved project steps,
up my neck and softly through widened nostrils
making it ever so impossible
to resist
the hunger within my swollen core.
Poplar Grove Evermore.
Saturday morning cartoons bloom
and police sirens zoom outside catching hideaways and runaways
I used to play with . . .
Sleep drags me back to lumpy sheets and separate heartbeats
of little cousins' arms and legs sharing the covers on a
broken bunkbed.
Poplar Grove Evermore . . .
drifting again until I hear so clear
Big Momma in the kitchen humming Negro hymns,
my eyes heavy with sand until sleep rules again.

Chapter Twenty-Two

My Visceral Heartbeat
The Hip-Hop Side of Me

At forty-nine years of age, I find I have outgrown many of the things I once enjoyed. And yet, even at the ripe old age of forty-nine, hip-hop still represents a primary, visceral side of me—the side of me that is unapologetically black, loud, and outspoken. Cocky, even. You see, dear reader, that is what hip-hop does to me. It shakes me from my middle-aged slumber and takes me back to the exhilaration of my youth, back to the metallic rattle and click of the D.C. subway I rode to high school. Back to those days when I pulled my black baseball cap over my darkened eyes. Back to when my headphones ceaselessly reverberated in my ears. Back to the sun shining on my sweaty face as I sprinted up and down an outdoor basketball court. Hip-hop takes me back, back to the moments of social upheaval which defined my adolescent epoch and the feelings of personal power that urged me to speak out—to scream out loud. When I hear hip-hop, I feel a shift within me. A tectonic, rolling movement that tells me, rhythmically, to walk with a strut and tilt my head to the side, to furrow my brow, to tap into that easy laconic cool that seems to fasten itself to the cellular makeup of dark skin, nappy hair, tumescent lips, saggy jeans, and black boots—swagger! I will always love this music. And there is nothing I can do about it. Hip-hop takes me to the gut-level of myself, down inside, where emotion is king.

Although there are countless forms and styles germane to hip-hop, my visceral side seems to crave sociopolitical hip-hop, conscious rap; the kind of rap which places the nation on the proverbial witness stand, unabashedly challenging the morality of the country's economic, legal, and cultural agendas, the kind of rap that screams in the face of America's missteps and broken promises. And so, I lean toward the effectual lamentations of Tupac Shakur. For me, Tupac's genius is unmatched in the hip-hop community. Tupac was special. He was the modern and more masculine version of James Baldwin, telling stories that define the depths of black struggle but doing so with a brazenfaced compassion and panache for insolence. That dude had chutzpa. He was a walking, talking detonation of talent and intellectual street tenacity. While Baldwin's work cleverly uncovered black reality through a myriad of black male characters (Leo Proudhammer of *Tell Me How Long the Train's Been Gone* and Fonny of *If Beale Street Could Talk*), Tupac's narratives characterized a more modern demographic. Yes, the narratives clearly tussled with similar plots, but Baldwin was about *then*. Tupac is about *now*. Even twenty years after his death, Tupac's songs still resonate, focusing heavily on young black men living in the 1980s and 90s; the young black men who were dealing with the fallout from Reaganomics, the war on drugs, the Gulf War, the crack epidemic, AIDS, and the like, the era to which I belong—the era of *displaced adulation.*

The power of Tupac, though, cannot not be discussed without recognizing the way he so brilliantly conjoined his outspoken charismatic brashness with a keen sense of black intellectualism. Anyone who listened to Tupac knew he was well read, yet being well read is only part of what made him great. Tupac's greatness had to do with the way he actualized his knowledge to tap into the widespread psychological desperation germane to black inner-city poverty. He did more than simply understand black life; he brought black life to the ears and minds of millions, and he did so without hubris. He put the truth in the listener's face, challenging the status quo with keen astuteness. His lyrics reminded my generation of the reasons why young black men so often turned to drugs as a means for self-pacification. His purpose was not to glorify such acts but simply to explain the reasons why these acts came to fruition. His purpose was to take the listener on a journey into the concrete wilderness, thereby highlighting the burgeoning state of nihilism in the black community. When one listens to Tupac, one becomes painfully aware of what black hopelessness looks like, of what optimism looks like, the ups and down of blackness. A listener becomes aware of why being black and male is often too much to take…too much to cope with. Tupac brought the truth.

When I close my eyes, I can hear him even now. He is pulsating through my headphones as I ride a city bus to high school. He is blasting through the speakers in my first car as I cruise toward the basketball courts in the heat of summer. He is thumping through the speakers in my first apartment as I sit on the balcony and stare at the traffic. He is with me at college as I walk through a mass of students heading to class. He is at my wedding reception as my family dances to "I Get Around." He is with me posthumously, even today, as I head toward middle age, living a life replete with wife and kids, with work and bills, with pressure and stress, doing what I can do. He is still here.

Can you hear him riding the beat as if it were an enraged bull, galloping atop the high heat, slurring his words at the end of his sentences, and spitting furious heat through his social commentary all while standing shirtless, tatted up, and mocking the hypocrisy of the system?

I can hear him even now as I cruise toward the University of Maryland to teach a class on Organizational Behavior while pulling into the parking lot beside my peers and other professors, professors who snarl at my choice of music, wondering why I am not playing classical or light jazz, rock or opera. No, that's not for me; give me more. I need the running commentary from the mind of a street poet, the one with the bandana and black shades, the one with the offensive gait and political wordplay, the one with the crooked smile, the one not afraid to uncover the truth about being young and black and fired up. "Can you hear him?"

Index

accomplishments: fighting back with, 20, 46; as genetic, 98; of Obama, 103, 107, 111; oversimplification of, 48; respect for, 82, 99
Afraprovidential, 48
Afroprovidential: on marijuana, 50–53; redirection grace and Black males, 45, 47–49, 52–53, 89
Afro-trepidationists, 103–4
Americans. *See* United States
anti-afrotraitism, 97–100
anti-intellectuals, 103
anti-trailblazer, 65
ascension of desires continuum, 88–94

Baldwin, James, 69, 117–18
Bandura, Albert, 59, 78
Barry, Marion, 99–100
basketball: as anti-trailblazer, 65; as average, 66–67; on Black intellectuals, 58–59, 64; Black safety and, 5; Blacks and, 3–5, 57–58; black scholastic ineptitude and, 68–69; for creativity and discipline, 57; for displaced adulation, 58–62, 64–69; hip-hop and, 117; slavery shackles and, 63–64; over street violence, 57; Whites and, 3–5

biracial: as Black or White, 55; children as, 19–20, 32–33, 45, 53, 76–77, 100; couple, 24, 76; ethnicities, 32; mixed-race family and, 24, 31–35
Black and White union: biracial couple in, 24, 76; Blacks on, 15–19, 34–35; circumstances of, 24; strangeness of, 23; wife appreciation in, 13–14, 17–20, 31, 33
Black collective, 91, 93
Black culture, 22–23, 83, 85, 89–90, 92
Black health, 91–92
Black inner-cognizance, 91, 94
Black intellectual: Afro-trepidationists on, 103–4; aspirations to, 14, 46, 61, 65, 69; basketball on, 58–59, 64; Obama as, 109; Shakur as, 118; U.S. on, 98
Black leaders: Blacks on, 33, 35, 105–6; as charismatic leaders, 98; Obama as, 97; racism on, 99–101; U.S. on, 97–99
Black Liberation Theology, 33
Black Lives Matter movement, 113
Black males: Afroprovidential redirection for, 45, 48–49, 52–53; anger of, 108; full regalia of, 43; greeting of, 32; as hunted, 39, 47, 51;

Index

as lazy, 81; saving of, 47–48; Shakur for, 118
Black psycho-efficacy, 93
Black reality, 39–40, 83, 118
Blacks: Afraprovidential and female, 48; archetypes and stereotypes on, 82; basketball and, 3–5, 57–58; biracial as White or, 55; on Black and White union, 15–19, 34–35; Black counterfeit personifications by, 48; Black justification by, 15–17; on Blackness, 74; business management lectures by, 11–13, 19–20, 27–28, 45–47; on bussing, 22–23; on bussing of schoolchildren, 22–23; Christian religion and, 20, 33; in competition, 15–19; connections and, 25; COVID-19 on, 112; culture of, 22–23, 83, 85, 89–90, 92; on education, 19, 46–47; education for, 13–15, 19; family for, 22; on fathers and children, 33; fear and power of, 104; food of, 23; free black will for, 25–26; full black man regalia of, 43; as girlfriends, 24; grace and, 45, 47–49, 52–53, 89; grand experiment not including, 82; growing up, 21–22, 46, 115; hip-hop and, 117–19; history of, 85; hopelessness of, 95, 118; as intellectual, 14, 46, 61, 65, 69; Maslow neglecting, 87; middle class and, 1–7, 20; motivation for, 88–93; as not monolith, 25; nuance of, 85; on Obama, 33, 35, 105–6; Out-Black-Me game on, 18–20; police on, 9–10; police on partying, 50–52; prison road crews as, 11; professor as, 12–13, 19–20, 27–28, 46–47; protective pessimism by, 106–7; pushing back, 27–28; race and childhood memories of, 1–4; as racially progressive, 103; racial reality and, 39–41, 74; racial reality intelligence and, 40–41; on racism, 6–7; reality of, 39–40, 83, 118; religion and, 20, 33, 89–90; running by, 6–7, 9–10; self-efficacy for, 59, 93, 102–3; smells and, 14, 21–22, 24; survival as, 22–23; truth of, 39–42, 47, 83; twoness in Whiteness and, 29, 95; uppity and, 102–3; U.S. on police and, 93, 113, 115; violence and physicality of, 39, 108; violence on, 58–59; Washington on, 42, 104; "the way I want to be," 71; Whites and selling out by, 15–16; Whites disqualified by, 18–19; Zombie Zeitgeist on, 43
Black safety: basketball and, 5; desires for, 91–93
Black truth, 41–42; on anger and animalism, 39, 47; Black reality as, 40; bottom hole as, 83; as perception, 39; as prison industrial complex, 39–40
Black workers, 82; displaced talent of, 85; Four Ideals model and, 84–86; motivation lack for, 83–85; motivation of, 84, 87–94; psychology of, 85; from slavery, 83, 87; unemployment rates of, 86
Brown, Claude, 21
Brown, James, 63
Brown, Walter, 40
business management lectures, 11–13, 19–20, 27–28, 45–47

Castile, Philando, 40, 113
children: as biracial, 19–20, 32–33, 45, 53, 76–77, 100; Blacks on fathers and, 33; Black youth and, 1, 45, 47; bussing of school, 22–23; education and reading by, 21
Christianity, 20, 33
Clark, Jamar, 40
classical conditioning, 78–79
cognitive acceleration, 66
COVID-19, 112–13
Crutcher, Terence, 113
culturemorbus, 88, 91–92

De Large, Robert, 99
desires, 79, 90; ascension of desires continuum as, 88–94; for Black collective, 91, 93; for Black health, 91–92; as Black inner-cognizance, 91, 94; for Black psycho-efficacy, 93; for Black safety, 91–93
DID. *See* dissociative identity disorder
A Different Mirror (Takaki), 81
diligence: on academics, 46; White males manipulating, 81–82, 86–87
displaced adulation: as anti-trailblazer, 65; basketball for, 58–62, 64–69; definition of, 58–59; on education, 60, 62–64; on emotions, 59–61; era of, 118; by humankind, 66; knowledge against, 65; low confidence and, 59; power of, 60; on regular persons, 58–60, 62, 64–69; Shakur and, 118; social images and, 62, 64–65; true potential after, 67
dissociation: definition of, 95; human togetherness vs., 95–96
dissociative identity disorder (DID), 97, 104; legitimacy denied for, 100–101, 105; personalities in, 105–9; personality dysfunction in, 96; of U.S., 101–2, 112
Dixon, Sheila, 100
DNA: accomplishments as, 98; learning and, 73, 75; as shared, 2, 75, 77; as White, 2
drugs, 48, 118; as marijuana, 50–53
Du Bois, W. E. B., 29, 67–68
DuBose, Sam, 40, 113

education: Black professor in, 12–13, 19–20, 27–28, 46–47; for Blacks, 13–15, 19; Black scholastic ineptitude on, 68–69; Blacks on, 19, 46–47; bureaucratic, sexist influences on, 68; childhood reading and, 21; cognitive acceleration and, 66; diligence on, 46; diplomas of, 12, 19, 27, 46, 67, 103; against displaced adulation, 65; displaced adulation on, 60, 62–64; institutionalized racism and, 19, 68; knowledge via, 67–68; as medicine, 65; Plato on, 67; as power, 103; race and lack of, 73; slaves and reading, 102–3; for societal demise, 70; students and, 45; talented tenth and, 68; as transcendent, 69–70; wealth of mind and, 68; as Whiteness, 15. *See also* learning
Einstein, Albert, 68
elders: impudence on, 19, 50; reverence on, 48–49
Elliott, Robert, 99
emotions: displaced adulation influencing, 59–61; hedonistic theory and, 60, 79; Lynch strategy on, 103
ethno-excommunication, 80

fighting back: with accomplishments, 20, 46; with fists, 16–17
Floyd, George, 40, 113
Four Ideals model (4M Ideal), 84–86
Franklin, Aretha, 63, 99
free black will, 25–26
full black man regalia, 43

Garner, Eric, 40
Gaston, A.G., 42
Gaye, Marvin, 21, 63
grace, 45, 47–49, 52–53, 89
grand experiment, 82
Gray, Freddie, 40, 113

hair: as afro, 22; as blond, 4, 20; as Hawaiian-like, 45; as nappy curls, 1, 6, 117; as straight, 2; as tightly curled, 24; tumescent afro, 31; as wild, 23
Harlow, Harry, 96
Harris, Eric, 40, 113
hedonistic theory, 60, 79
Hendricks, Barkley, 21

Heron, Gill Scott, 21
hierarchy model, 87–91
hip-hop, 117–19
historically black college, 24
hopelessness, 95, 118

intelligence: basketball on, 58–59, 64; definition of, 40; on race, 40; racial knowledge as cultural, 41; students with, 73; types of, 40; "the way I want to be" and, 71

Jefferson, Thomas, 41
Johnson, James Weldon, 21
Joplin, Janis, 23

Kilpatrick, Kwame, 100

Lacks, Henrietta, 42
leadership theory, 97–98
learning: anti-intellectuals on, 103; from basketball, 57; commitment to, 19, 28, 68–69; DNA and, 73, 75; intelligence and, 40; from peer group, 77–78; power of high-level, 66–68, 71, 104; race and, 41, 75, 77–78, 80; for self, 59–60; social acceptance and, 80; social learning theory and, 77–79; society with race, 41; from thinkers, 66–67, 70; US citizen dissociated from, 96. *See also* education
Long, Jefferson Franklin, 99
Lucian, John, 21
Lynch, Willy, 103

malignant narcissism, 112
marginalized ideal, 84, 86
Marley, Bob, 14, 35, 63
Maslow, Abraham, 45, 87–91
master narrative, 81–82, 85–86
McDole, Jeremy, 40
middle class, 1–7, 20
misappropriated ideal, 84–86
misdiagnosed ideal, 84–86
misunderstood ideal, 84–86
mixed-race family, 24, 31–35
Monk, Thelonious, 45
motivation: ascension of desires continuum and, 91–94; Black culture, ascension and employee, 22–23, 83, 85, 89–90, 92; of Black employees, 84, 87–94; for Blacks, 88–93; on culturemorbus, 88, 91–92; hiring vs. employee, 86; inner-cognizance and, 91, 94; lack of employee, 83–85; of learning, 79; Maslow and, 87–88
Muddy Waters, 63

narcissistic personality disorder (NPD), 112–14

Obama, Barack: accomplishments of, 103, 107, 111; anti-afrotraitism and leadership of, 97; as Black intellectual, 109; Blacks on, 33, 35, 105–6; DID types on, 97, 100–101, 105; era of, 111; presidential legitimacy of, 105; ultra-conservative and super-liberal for, 107; Whites on, 101–2, 104–8; women issues on, 107–8
operant conditioning, 79–80
Out-Black-Me game, 18–20

parenting: elder respect by, 48–49; race and, 76–77; as single, 48; for value system, 58, 62–63
Pavlov, Ivan, 78–80
peer group: as Black, 16; as desirable, 75; learning from, 77–78; racial learning and, 78; as young, 49, 52, 61
Plato, 67
police: on Blacks, 9–10; on partying, 50–52; son and fear of, 24; U.S. on Blacks and, 93, 113, 115; violence and, 39–40, 93; "the way I want to be" and, 71
Poplar Grove Evermore, 115

power: of DID, 101; of displaced adulation, 60; education as, 103; fear on Blacks and, 104; free will and, 25–26; as higher, 49; of high-level thought, 66–68, 71, 104; from hip-hop, 117–18; of nonviolence, 20; of president, 107, 109; on racial categories, 76, 81; Whites with, 27–28, 81, 103
presidential, 105, 107, 109, 113
prison industrial complex: Afroprovidential on Black males and, 45, 48–49, 52–53; Black road crews of, 11; Black truth as, 39–40; students vs. road crews of, 14
protective pessimism, 106–7
psycho-efficacy, 93

race: Americans on, 73; Black childhood memories of, 1–4; as categorization, 41, 55; classical conditioning and, 78–79; definition of, 74; DNA and, 2, 75, 77; ethno-excommunication and, 80; eyesight on, 74–75; after fourteenth century, 76; as impenetrable wall, 101; intelligence on, 40; learning and, 41, 75, 77–78, 80; Maslow model on, 87; miseducation on, 73; of multiracial parentage, 19–20, 32–33, 45, 53, 76–77, 100; Obama and DID on, 97, 100–101, 105; operant conditioning and, 79–80; power and categories of, 76, 81; progressiveness on, 103; social untruths on, 73; stereotypes and, 73; "the way I want to be" and, 71; Whites and progressive on, 103
racial knowledge, 41
racial mythologies, 73
racial reality, 39–41, 74
racial reality intelligence, 40–41
racism: on Black leaders, 99–101; Blacks dealing with, 6–7; charismatic leaders as, 98; education and institutionalized, 19, 68; by Whites, 4–6
rage, 7, 16–18, 34
Ransier, Alonzo, 99
Rapier, James, 99
regular persons: displaced adulation on, 58–60, 62, 64–69; significance of, 59
religion: Black Liberation Theology as, 33; Black people and, 89–90; Blacks and Christian, 20, 33
Rice, Tamir, 40, 113

Scott, Walter, 40, 113
self-efficacy, 59, 93, 102–3
Shakur, Tupac, 117–19
Simone, Nina, 21
Skinner, B.F., 79–80
skin tone: as bronze, 21, 100; as brown clay, 53; as brown-tones, 12–13; as caramel, 45; as caste system, 103; as coffee, 100; as dark, 29, 32, 117; as honey brown, 24, 61; as ink, 27–28, 31; as mahogany, 11; as milky white, 31–32; as moonstone, 2; as obsidian, 31; as onyx, 31, 62; as pale, freckled, 3, 20; as tan, 13; as tar and licorice, 63; as tree bark, 14; violence on brown, 58–59; as warm clay, 31; as whiteness, 5, 15, 27
slavery: basketball and, 63–64; Black workers from, 83, 87; destinations of, 42; Lynch and psycho-emotional strategy on, 103; reading and, 102–3; steps of, 37; uppity and, 102–3; Washington and, 42, 104
social learning theory, 77–79
society: displaced adulation for, 62, 64–65; dissociation vs., 95–96; education for demise and, 70; knowledge and barricades of, 65; learning and acceptance in, 80; learning theory and, 77–79; race and untruths of, 73
soul food, 23
Spencer, Herbert, 99

Sterling, Alton, 40
street poet, 117–19
suburbia, 1–7, 20

Takaki, Ronald, 81
talented tenth, 68
tea party, 104, 108
trait theory, 97–98
Traoré, Adama, 113
Trump, Donald J., 112–13
Tulsa race riots, 42
twoness, 29, 95

United States (U.S.): anti-afrotraitism by Whites and, 100; on Black intellectualism, 98; on Black leaders, 97–99; Black role in, 41–42; on Blacks and police, 93, 113, 115; DID and, 101–2, 112; DID on Obama, 97, 100–101, 105; grand experiment of, 82; learning dissociation in, 96; master narrative of, 81–82, 85–86; on presidential power, 107, 109; on race, 73; on racial reality intelligence, 40–41; trait approach in, 97–98
uppity, 102–3
U.S. *See* United States

value systems, 58, 62–63
violence: basketball over street, 57; on black and brown bodies, 58–59; Black physicality and, 39, 108; nonviolence and, 20; of police, 39–40, 93

Washington, George, 42, 104
"the way I want to be," 71
wealth of mind, 68
West, Cornel, 66
White males: master narrative of, 81–82, 85–86; trait theory on, 98
Whiteness: education as, 15; as relatively acceptable, 23; twoness in Blackness and, 29, 95; Whites on, 74
Whites: anti-afrotraitism by, 100; basketball and, 3–5; biracial as Black or, 55; Black counterfeit personifications by, 48; Blacks disqualifying, 18–19; Blacks selling out to, 15–16; COVID-19 on, 113; DNA and, 2; on Obama, 101–2, 104–8; with power, 27–28, 81, 103; as racially progressive, 103; racism by, 4–6; on Whiteness, 74
women: Afraprovidential for Black, 48; grand experiment not including, 82; on Obama, 107–8

Zombie Zeitgeist, 43

About the Author

Bernard Grenway holds a Bachelor of Liberal Studies from the University of Maine at Presque Isle, a Graduate Certificate of Executive Leadership from Cornell University, a Master of Science in Human Relations from Amberton University, and a MBA and PhD in Applied Management. He is currently working on a second Doctoral Degree in Education at Maryville University. Dr. Grenway is an Associate Adjunct Professor at the University of Maryland Global Campus and a Professor of Business at the American National University. He is also the author of *Random Musings: Reflections of a Black Intellectual* and his work has been published in academic research journals such as the Journal of Sociology and Religion.

www.ingramcontent.com/pod-product-compliance
Lightning Source LLC
Chambersburg PA
CBHW020419230426
43663CB00007BA/1241